C ..... and ..... Plants

CASSELL'S DIRECTORY OF

Courtyard and Patio Plants

EVERYTHING YOU NEED TO CREATE A GARDEN

JANE COURTIER

Consultant Editor
LUCY HUNTINGTON

CASSELL&CO

First published in the United Kingdom in 2000 by CASSELL & CO

Design and text copyright © The Ivy Press Limited 2000

A CIP Catalogue record for this book
is available from the British Library

ISBN 0 304 35943 2

This book was conceived,
designed and produced by
THE IVY PRESS LIMITED
The Old Candlemakers, West Street,
Lewes, East Sussex BN7 2NZ

Creative Director: PETER BRIDGEWATER
Designers: AXIS DESIGN
Editorial Director: DENNY HEMMING
Managing Editor: ANNE TOWNLEY
Illustrations: VANESSA LUFF & PETER BULL
Picture Researcher: LIZ EDDISON

Originated and printed by
Hong Kong Graphic, Hong Kong

This book is typeset in Linotype Perpetua and Univers

CASSELL & CO
Wellington House, 125 Strand, London WC2R 0BB

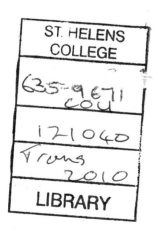

CONTENTS

INTRODUCTION

Patio and courtyard gardens tend to be intimate areas, designed for enjoyment – eating, entertaining or simply sitting – and more than any other type of garden they are for using and living in, not just for admiring from afar. On warm summer evenings and at weekends these areas come into their own, providing valuable additional space – an 'outdoor room' – in which to relax. Their relatively sheltered position extends their season of use into spring and autumn, more than repaying the expense of creating the area.

The word 'patio' derives from the Latin *spatium* (space), something which is often a rare commodity in today's crowded world. A patio garden can provide us with the space we need to relax, and in towns and cities especially, where space is at a premium, a small patio garden or court-yard can be an ideal retreat.

Turning a patio into a patio garden means growing a far wider and more interesting range of plants than the stalwart old favourites that can seen in their thousands in windowboxes, tubs and hanging baskets across the country. There are literally dozens of beautiful and practical containers in a variety of materials to choose from at any reasonably sized garden centre, and there is an even greater selection of wonderful plants available to fill them. More permanent situations such as raised beds also give scope

for imaginative planting. Trees and shrubs, climbers and trailers, alpines, perennials and bedding plants can be used to fill the patio garden with colour and interest the whole year round. A sheltered area, where plants can more easily receive individual attention, will also give you the opportunity to try out some really special, choice plants that require protection from the elements. These may be just a bit more difficult to grow successfully than their run-of-the-mill relations, but they will give you the kind of spectacular results that will make you the envy of all your neighbours.

However, there is more to making a patio garden than just laying some paving slabs and adding a few pots of bedding plants. Factors such as choosing the right situation, deciding on the most appropriate surface and providing shelter and privacy have to be considered, and the surface and its surrounds must be properly constructed to ensure that the area is trouble free. You also need to think about the needs of the people using the garden.

LEFT *Containers are perfect for patio gardens. They are ideal for increasing the available planting area, and can be used for permanent plants and temporary seasonal additions.*

A GARDEN FOR ENJOYMENT

Some people are put off gardening by the amount of work involved. Because patio gardens are relatively small, they are easier to care for than a larger garden, where there are always jobs that need to be done and where gardening can become something of a chore. This is an important consideration if you have a busy lifestyle, because you are unlikely to find your garden relaxing if it is simply a further source of work. Patio gardens may also be appropriate for elderly or disabled people who enjoy gardening but who do not have the energy to devote to maintaining a large area. A stroll around a warm patio on a summer evening, with a glass of wine in one hand and a pair of secateurs in the other, can be a time of pure pleasure. Patios have their place in larger gardens, too, providing secluded, sheltered areas from where it is possible to sit and relax while admiring the view offered by the rest of the garden.

This book will guide you through the whole process of creating a patio or courtyard garden, from planning and constructing a new feature from scratch to renovating and improving an existing area. The focus of the book is on the range and variety of plants that are appropriate for patio gardens. The comprehensive directory of plants will give you a host of ideas for filling your new garden with flowers and foliage, and straightforward, easy-to-follow information on the preferences of each plant will make sure that whatever species you choose will thrive and remain healthy. There is also advice on laying the foundations for a good patio garden and creating the right situation for the plants you want to grow.

With the help of this book you will be able to make the perfect garden retreat for yourself and your family.

ABOVE *The desire to create a pleasant place to sit and relax is usually the main impetus for building a patio garden.*

HOW TO USE THIS BOOK

*C*assell's Garden Directories have been conceived and written to appeal both to gardening
beginners and to confident gardeners who need advice for a specific project. Each book
focuses on a particular type of garden, drawing on the experience of an established expert.
The emphasis is on a practical and down-to-earth approach that takes account of the space,
time and money that you have available. The ideas and techniques in these books will help
you to produce an attractive and manageable garden that you will enjoy for years to come.

Cassell's Directory of Courtyard and Patio Plants looks at the
kinds of plants you can grow in limited space in town
gardens, and the options for creating an all-weather area
in a more substantial garden. The book is divided into three
sections. The opening section, *Planning Your Garden*, explains
the advantages of patio gardening, and looks at some of
the problems that you may need to overcome. There are
also three specific inspirational garden plans for producing
a shady garden, a garden for easy maintenance and a
container garden for an enclosed courtyard.

Part Two of the book, *Creating Your Garden*, moves on
to the nitty-gritty of putting your ideas into practice. This
section opens with some advice on the range of different
surfaces that you can choose from, and on selecting water
features such as fountains and pools. There is also information on selecting and planting appropriate shrubs, herbs
and flowers, as well as finding imaginative containers that
can be used to create a fragrant corner.

The remainder of Part Two is packed with practical
information on basic techniques, such as laying different
surfaces, sowing, feeding and weeding, and supporting and
pruning plants. Moving on from this basic grounding, this
section then encourages you to put your skills to work with
a series of specific projects such as building raised beds and
creating a water garden. There are step-by-step illustrations throughout this section that show clearly and simply
what you need to do to achieve the best results. Also
included are handy hints and tips, points to watch out for,
and star plants that are particularly suitable for the projects
that are described.

The final part of the book, *The Plant Directory*, is a
comprehensive listing of all the plants mentioned in the
earlier sections, together with other plants that are suitable for a patio garden. Each plant is illustrated, and there
is complete information on appropriate growing conditions, speed of growth, and ease of maintenance.

GARDEN SCHEMES are
included to inspire you
to great things in your
own garden.

COLOUR PHOTOGRAPHS
show what can be
achieved with a little
effort and imagination.

3D PLANS show the
best planting scheme
for you to achieve the
ideal outcome.

THE KEY FEATURES of
the plan are described
to help you visualize
the final effect.

CHOICES SPREADS show a selection of plants, garden furniture or other features that might be appropriate in your garden.

THE CHECKLIST details important things to look out for in choosing garden features.

COLOUR PHOTOGRAPHS help you to decide on the appropriate feature for your garden.

EXPLANATORY TEXT describes the various possibilities available in each category.

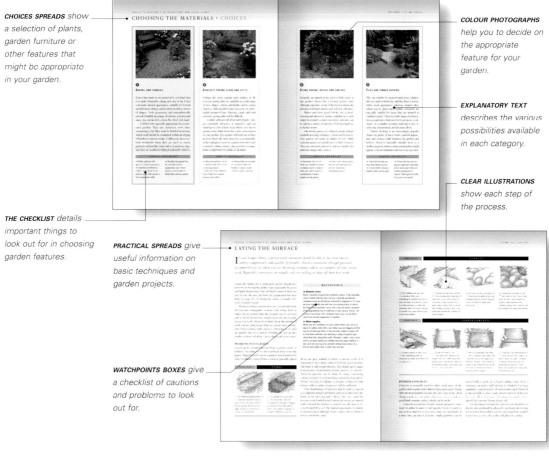

PRACTICAL SPREADS give useful information on basic techniques and garden projects.

WATCHPOINTS BOXES give a checklist of cautions and problems to look out for.

CLEAR ILLUSTRATIONS show each step of the process.

THE PLANT DIRECTORY is organized into categories, making it simple to find a particular type of plant.

COLOUR PHOTOGRAPHS clearly identify each plant listed.

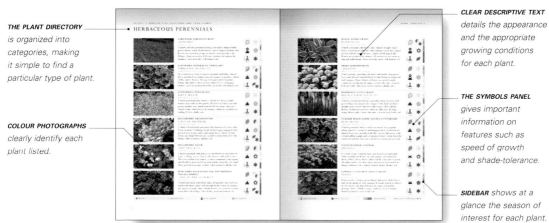

CLEAR DESCRIPTIVE TEXT details the appearance and the appropriate growing conditions for each plant.

THE SYMBOLS PANEL gives important information on features such as speed of growth and shade-tolerance.

SIDEBAR shows at a glance the season of interest for each plant.

9

PLANNING YOUR GARDEN

1

An 'outside room' has to be carefully planned – it is not simply a matter of cramming as many pots into an area as possible, but rather the careful selection of a few choice items for maximum impact. This section surveys all the ingredients of a good patio garden and provides a troubleshooting guide to help you overcome problems such as a lack of sunlight and privacy. Finally, should you have the energy to start from scratch, the section concludes with three complete patio plans for you to try out.

LEFT *In this rectangular courtyard, a quartet of conifers in tubs and a central water feature all combine to create a highly formal effect.*

WHAT IS A PATIO GARDEN?

A patio, a paved or hard-surfaced area, usually adjoining the house, is quite different from a patio garden. A patio may be wholly functional: a place to enjoy a meal out of doors on fine days or somewhere the children can play without getting too muddy. A patio garden, on the other hand, suggests a secluded, self-contained area, filled with plants.

The main characteristic distinguishing the patio garden from other types of garden is that it has a hard surface and little or no natural soil in which to grow plants. There may be soil below the surface, to which it is sometimes possible to gain access by breaking up small areas to create planting pockets, but these represent only a small proportion of the whole garden. It is often, however, neither possible nor practicable to expose the existing soil, and in any case, its quality may be so poor that nothing will thrive in it. If this is the case, don't panic, because a host of options still remains open to you. Plants in patio gardens are grown in containers, which are usually filled with imported soil. Raised beds are another feature of many patio gardens.

Built on the patio's surface, such beds are extra-large containers, which can be planted with a wider range of plants than can be grown in tubs and pots.

IDEALLY SITUATED

A patio garden may well be the entire garden area attached to a house. This is common in towns, where land is too valuable to allow much of it to be spared for gardens. A small, often narrow, paved area at the back of the house does not, at first sight, hold much promise, but it can be turned into a luxuriant patio garden. The patio garden also has a place within the larger garden, however. Such an area is usually directly next to the house, which may have French windows or even patio doors for ease of access, and in such circumstances it can form a valuable outdoor room, providing an opportunity to create an entirely different kind of atmosphere from the remainder of the garden. A patio garden is generally small because of practicality and

LEFT *Tonal contrasts are often particularly effective in small areas: here dark 'Queen of Night' tulips are enhanced by a pale-flowered backdrop of 'Francis E. Lester' roses.*

cost but, in any case, a large expanse of a hard surface such as concrete has a harsh, unwelcoming appearance. If you do have a large area to cover, use sympathetic materials and furnish liberally with containers.

CONSERVING PRIVACY

Although many patio gardens are partially enclosed, they can be completely open, especially if there is a view to be appreciated. It is, however, usual to have a screen to provide privacy, frequently a wall or fence butting up at right angles to the house wall to form a sheltered corner.

ABOVE *Here a selection of foliage plants, highlighted by a few white and yellow flowers, creates a cool, restful retreat away from the bustle of the outside world.*

A courtyard garden differs only slightly from a patio garden, and many people use both terms to mean the same thing. Originally, a courtyard was a central, open space, surrounded on all sides by buildings. In some countries the surrounding buildings formed the residential rooms of the house; in other countries the courtyard was more likely to be surrounded by stables. It had a regular shape, often with a central feature, such as a tree or fountain.

A courtyard garden has a hard surface and it usually has a formal design and appearance. Although often attached to a grand house, it may also be a feature of a smaller dwelling, particularly in a town where neighbouring houses provide the surrounding walls. Shade may be a problem in such a garden, but the walls provide shelter, which is usually welcome.

POINTS TO CONSIDER

🍃 For maximum value and ease of use, a patio garden should be easily accessible from the house.

🍃 Think of a patio garden as an extra room, giving as much consideration to the layout, decoration and furnishings as you would to the interior of the house.

THE ADVANTAGES OF PATIO GARDENING

There are many reasons why a patio or courtyard garden will prove an asset to your home: it will enhance the appearance of your house, create a firm, dry area for wet days and also provide additional space for choice plants. A well-designed and executed patio will, almost certainly, increase the value of your property, although that is unlikely to be your overriding motive.

A paved area can look attractive, especially when it is furnished with appropriate plants, but even on its own, paving and other hard surfaces can be a valuable design feature, adding interest and introducing variety to the garden. Dull, shady gardens, where there is little natural light, can benefit enormously from light-coloured surfaces, which reflect what light there is to brighten the whole area.

Situated as it normally is immediately adjacent to the house, a patio garden forms an important link between the wider garden and the home. Patio doors or French windows will help to emphasize the connection, and even when it is not in use, a well-planned patio will form a pleasing outlook from the windows of the house. Attractive pots, statues and ornaments can all be used as embellishments, and make it possible for a flair for interior design to be used outdoors. The smaller scale might also encourage home-owners who do not have an extensive knowledge of plants and gardening and who might feel intimidated by the thought of full-scale garden design.

CONVENIENCE

A paved area has one major benefit over other types of surface: it is dry underfoot. A patio garden can be used immediately after rain, when lawns would be too wet to walk on without proper waterproof shoes. Most types of patio surface are easy to sweep clean, helping to avoid the problem of mud, leaves and general garden dirt being carried into the house.

BELOW *This low-maintenance patio combines brick and timber to stunning effect.*

ABOVE *Dwarf bulbs are a natural choice for patio gardens, and in a sheltered climate may flower earlier than elsewhere.*

A patio also provides a practical surface for garden furniture, as it is level and firm, so that there is no danger of chairs and tables sinking into soft earth or tipping over. It is an ideal place for children to play. The hard surface may not be as forgiving as grass when it comes to tumbles, but it is perfect for wheeled toys and helps to avoid muddy shoes and grass-stained clothes. Stable table and chairs can be used for eating, drawing and reading, encouraging children to stay out in the fresh air instead of returning indoors. When the patio is near the house, the children will be close at hand so that it is easier to keep a watchful eye on them. At the other end of the age range, elderly and infirm gardeners generally find paved areas easier and safer to move around on.

In densely populated areas many gardens are overlooked to some extent. The use of evergreen and climbing plants as screens, together with a plant-draped pergola, gives seclusion without being offensive to neighbours.

HINTS AND TIPS

- White or light-coloured paving materials will help to brighten a dull or shady patio, but can be uncomfortably glaring for an area in full sun.
- Use weatherproof garden furniture that does not need to be brought under cover in case of rain; this will encourage you to use the patio more frequently.
- Make use of evergreens, ornaments and sculpture to ensure the patio looks attractive through the winter as well as the summer.

POINTS TO CONSIDER

- In hot, sunny weather, some light shade is valuable on a small area of the patio to make sitting out more comfortable.
- A patio forms a link between the house and garden, so choose construction materials that blend pleasingly with the fabric of the house.
- Deciduous climbing plants form a screen to give privacy in summer, but shed their leaves to allow plenty of light to the patio in winter, when seclusion is not so important.
- Make sure sufficient priority is given to providing proper drainage; paved surfaces can be very easily flooded.

CLIMATE

In cool climates, most patio gardens are constructed where they will catch the maximum amount of sun. By using hard surfaces to reflect back the heat and maximizing the shelter provided by the walls, your use of the patio can be extended at both ends of the season, allowing the garden to be enjoyed earlier in spring and later in autumn.

The shelter and warmth also allow an increased range of plants to be grown, and these sometimes come into season earlier because of the favourable climate. Spring-flowering plants grown in a sheltered patio garden will often make their appearance several weeks before they are seen in less well-protected gardens. If your garden is generally very hot and sunny, on the other hand, you may want to site the patio on the coolest side of the house. Shade-producing plants and screens can be used to protect the area from the sun, creating a leafy, dappled shade that will provide a wonderfully cool and relaxing place to retreat to in the fierce heat of a summer's day.

SURFACE DESIGNS

The pattern and design of the patio garden surface should be established during the early planning stages, as it may affect the overall shape and size of the garden. The many possibilities are limited mainly by budget and by ease of construction if you are doing the work yourself. Before you select your surfacing material, draw an accurate scale plan of the area. This will make it relatively simple to estimate the cost.

Paving slabs are available in a wide range of shapes and sizes which can be combined to form attractive formal and informal patterns. In a small area, the number of different sized slabs used should normally be limited to three to avoid the pattern becoming unnecessarily complicated, with an over-fussy appearance. As well as rectangular and square slabs, there are hexagons, to give a honeycomb effect, and various-sized 'segments', to enable round areas of paving to be created. Slabs are also available with patterns pressed into the surface to give the effect of setts, crazy paving or bricks; these need to be laid very carefully to minimize the appearance of the joints between slabs.

It is not usual to mix different sizes of bricks or paviors in a surface, but they can be laid in a variety of different patterns. Herringbone is a popular brick pattern, but traditional herringbone requires large numbers of bricks to be cut to form a straight edge. Basket-weave, parquet or right-angle herringbone patterns overcome this problem, using only whole bricks; this makes the job much quicker and easier, and avoids wastage through spoiled bricks. Some paviors are manufactured in an angled or indented shape, which forms a zigzag pattern when laid.

At its simplest, timber decking uses planks laid parallel to the edges of the plot. A more striking effect can be achieved by using planks diagonally across the site (though this does involve more cutting of timber), and an attractive pattern can be obtained by laying areas of planks at right angles to each other. The most effective way to use timber tiles is to lay each tile with the wood running at right angles to its neighbour, forming a chequerboard pattern, though some have ready-made patterns within each tile. The drawback with this type of surface, however, is that it can become slippery after rainfall.

HINTS AND TIPS

- If you are laying the paving or patio surface yourself, keep the design fairly simple, and where possible avoid having to cut too many bricks and slabs.
- Be as accurate as you can when estimating the amount of materials needed for the job.
- Draw out a design to scale on squared paper before finalizing your plan.

LEFT *Striking effects can be achieved with the simplest designs: a gravel circle edged with brick highlights a feature container of* Zantedeschia aethiopica *surrounded by a tumble of* Glechoma hederacea *'Variegata'.*

Roman villa gardens were often decorated with attractive *trompe l'oeil* paintings on the walls of their courtyards, making the gardens appear larger than they were. Several well-preserved examples exist in the ruined city of Pompeii.

A straightforward way of achieving the same sort of effect is to use mirrors that will give the impression of extra plants and more room.

ABOVE *Consider surrounding features when selecting your patio material. Here, stone slabs have been chosen to complement the stone walls.*

USING COLOURS

Paving slabs do not only come in a mix of different shapes and sizes, but also in a range of colours. Slabs of different but toning colours can give attractive effects; use them to form patterns in the same way you would use different shapes and sizes of slabs. Very strong colour contrasts can prove wearing to the eye unless used carefully to form a small part of the design. Contrasting colours of bricks and paviors are often used to edge the paved area, but can also form decorative patterns within it.

Glazed ceramic tiles can be obtained in very strong, bright colours, which can be most striking in an outdoor setting, giving a Mediterranean ambience that is particularly welcome in cooler climates. However, strong colours should be used carefully. They are best limited to small areas, otherwise they can be visually disturbing and detract from the plant display. An area of glass tiles, usually in tones of blue or green, can give the appearance of moving water and can be very dramatic.

Gravel is straightforward to lay, simply being raked out evenly to cover the surface, but it is possible to achieve some very attractive effects by using areas of differently coloured gravel to form a pattern. Each area must be kept separate with a permanent edging such as bricks, tiles, timber or similar, which should be in place before any gravel is spread.

COMBINATION SURFACES

Some of the most effective patio gardens use surfaces that are a combination of two or three different types of material. Avoid using too many types in a small area — it will look bitty and fussy. Use different materials on a large scale — to mark out a sitting or dining area from the rest of the patio garden, for example — or on a smaller scale, to form a pattern running through the main surface. A material that is suitable for either indoors or outdoors, such as quarry tiles, helps achieve an effective transition from house to garden if used immediately outside patio doors, for example.

Bricks or paviors are often used to define the edges of an area of paving slabs; on a large expanse of slabs, paviors can also be used to divide the surface into rectangles, squares or diamonds. There are many different colours of paviors available to blend or contrast effectively with various shades of paving.

Gravel in a variety of shades forms an ideal 'background' surface in which to set timber decking tiles or stone slabs for an informal effect; occasional groups of cobblestones or larger, decorative boulders form a good link between gravel and stone slabs. One of the great advantages of gravel is that it can be used to fill out irregularly-shaped areas around the borders of the patio garden, which may be awkward to fill with less flexible materials.

PATIO GARDEN FEATURES

A *paved area, even when adorned with a few containers of plants, is not yet a patio garden. It needs a range of other features, including those below. You might also want to include raised beds (see pages 56–57) and a water feature (see pages 60–61).*

An open, paved area is just a patio, but some form of shelter will help to turn it into a patio garden. Small gardens and courtyards may be entirely surrounded by walls, often belonging to neighbouring properties.

If there are no existing walls, providing a sheltering wall need be neither expensive nor difficult, although you should seek professional advice for any wall that is over about 1m (3ft) high. A well-built wall will be virtually maintenance-free and will outlast both hedges and fences.

As with any hard landscaping material that you are considering introducing to the garden, take care when you select the style and type of walling. Make sure that it harmonizes both with the style of your garden and with the wider environment of your area. You must also ensure that the material is suitable for the purpose.

Screen block walling is comparatively inexpensive and easier to build than a solid wall. The style is not to everyone's taste, but the blocks can be disguised with climbing plants, and they have the advantage of allowing some privacy without excluding all light. The perforated blocks, which are available in a variety of geometric patterns, are usually supported at the ends and at intervals along the length by piers and reinforced with iron rods.

Brick is widely available and comparatively cheap. A versatile material, it is suitable for both formal and informal, urban and rural gardens. It can be laid in a variety of bonds and styles, and can also be combined with other materials and topped with wooden fencing.

Natural stone is a wonderful material for walls and is available in a wide variety of sizes and shades. Walling stone is supplied in irregular shapes and sizes (rough cut), shaped into more regular blocks (squared) or smoothly finished and cut into neat squares (ashlar). Alternatively, a dry-stone effect can be achieved by removing the mortar from the visible joints of a conventional, mortared wall.

POINTS TO CONSIDER

🍂 One of the most useful items for a small patio garden is a mirror, which both increases the feeling of space and also, when carefully positioned, gives an amusing *trompe l'oeil* effect. Special outdoor mirrors are available.

🍂 Some of the most attractive outdoor furniture is made from teak. Although it is expensive, this furniture is lovely to look at and will outlast many less costly items.

🍂 When you are erecting a panelled fence of whatever kind, do not be tempted to put all the posts in place first and then try to fit the panels between them – it is easy to get the mathematics wrong which will lead to disaster.

LEFT *A large umbrella creates a sheltered area that opens up a patio garden to use even if the weather is inclement. The umbrella can be put to one side on sunny days.*

FENCES

A much cheaper alternative to walls, fences are much quicker to erect, and modern pressure-treatment has given timber a longer life than in the past. The greatest privacy is provided by a simple fence of solid panels, which can be attached to timber or concrete posts. If you use timber posts, use metal post supports or concrete spurs, which will protect the bases from rot.

Trellis-work screens are light and quick to erect, and there are several unusual materials available, including heather, split canes and willow. Most of these materials have a life span of up to 15 years. An open-work fence allows air to circulate around the plants, which is an advantage.

ORNAMENTS

A beautiful statue or garden ornament will make a magnificent focal point in the patio garden, and ornaments do not need to be expensive. You could have a group of empty containers; an attractive piece of weathered stone; piles of smooth grey boulders or pebbles; 'antique' metal containers or watering cans from junk yards.

FURNITURE

The patio garden is a place to sit and relax, enjoying your surroundings. The provision of comfortable seating and a suitable table is, therefore, very important.

A sitting area with permanent furniture should be sited in the most sheltered part of the garden and the one with the best outlook. Steps and raised beds can be a useful way of providing extra seating, especially when you are entertaining. Make steps suitably wide for this purpose and provide an appropriate coping stone on top of the walls of raised beds. For comfort, the top of the raised bed needs to be at least 45cm (18in) high.

Permanent seating includes items such as stone seats and wooden or metal benches, which are left in position all year round. These will need regular cleaning and maintenance, and wooden furniture should be painted or coated with a suitable preservative, which will need to be renewed periodically. Choose wood, metal or resin furniture that will suit your pocket and the style of your garden.

ABOVE A pond or water feature will enhance the tranquillity of modern and traditional gardens, and continue to provide interest throughout the seasons.

OVERCOMING PROBLEMS

*S*ometimes difficulties arise that seem to make the creation of the perfect patio or courtyard garden unattainable, but very often, with a little creative planning, these can be overcome. Visiting other gardens to see how similar difficulties have been surmounted may be the only impetus you need, but the first step is to identify the problem.

If the problem is that you are on a tight budget and cannot afford to spend a lot of money on a patio garden, the key is to think ahead. Decide on the type of garden you would ultimately like to have and work out a plan for achieving it in stages. Choosing a cheaper surface – gravel or plain, cut-price paving slabs laid on a bed of sand, for example – will keep down the costs. This surface can be replaced with a more expensive material later on. Look in junk yards and at car-boot sales for unusual plant containers and garden ornaments and buy plants from charity sales and local markets rather than from garden centres.

SLOPES

You may have a garden that slopes steeply away from the house, leaving no space for a patio. It is possible to build a patio garden as a series of terraces, which are linked by shallow steps. The change in level adds interest to the design and gives a variety of different views.

This is also a possible solution if the garden slopes towards the house, but you must pay particular attention to the drainage in these circumstances and make sure that water drains away from the house.

SHADE

Sometimes houses are oriented so that the area immediately outside the patio doors is always in shade while the warmest, sunniest spot is at the other end of the garden. Remember that there is absolutely no rule to say that a patio garden has to be adjacent to your house. There are sometimes advantages to having a secluded area away from the comings and goings through the back door. Link your patio to the house with a path made from the same material used to surface the patio.

FROST POCKETS

If your garden is on a slope it is possible that the plants will be affected by frost. When you are choosing plants, remember that cold air, like water, flows downhill. If it is stopped part way down by a solid wall, the freezing air will collect against the obstacle and create a frost pocket. Solid walls should be built on the highest point of the slope to divert the air, while the boundary on the lower slope should be more open to allow the cold air to flow away.

SUNKEN YARD

If the only area available to you is a low, dark, basement yard, consider building your patio garden on two or three terraces. Use a light-coloured surfacing material and paint the surrounding walls in a light-coloured paint. Outdoor

LEFT *A patio sited at the top of a sloping garden uses the difference in level to advantage to create a more private area, with a curtain of tree branches and screening shrubs.*

STAR PLANTS

Shade-tolerant plants
- *Arum italicum* 'Marmoratum'
- *Aucuba japonica* 'Gold Dust'
- *Buxus sempervirens*
- *Camellia japonica*
- *Cotoneaster salicifolius* 'Pendulus'
- *Dicksonia antarctica*
- *Dodecatheon meadia*
- *Eranthis hyemalis*
- *Erythronium dens-canis*
- *Euonymus fortunei* 'Emerald 'n' Gold'
- *Fatsia japonica*
- *Fritillaria meleagris*
- *Galanthus nivalis*
- *Gaultheria mucronata*
- *Hedera helix* 'Oro di Bogliasco'
- *Helleborus argutifolius*
- *Ilex aquifolium* 'J.C. van Tol'
- *Mahonia aquifolium* 'Apollo'
- *Polystichum polyblepharum*
- *Pyracantha watereri*
- *Rhododendron* 'Kirin'
- *Sarcococca confusa*
- *Taxus baccata* 'Standishii'
- *Tolmiea menziesii*
- *Vinca major*
- *Vinca minor*

ABOVE *If the garden is very overlooked by neighbouring houses, a pergola clothed in climbers will add privacy.*

mirrors will help to capture the available light, and garden lighting will add atmosphere. Choose plants that will live happily in shady conditions (see box above). With a little imagination, you can create some dramatic effects.

LACK OF PRIVACY

Where patios are overlooked from upstairs windows a pergola with a 'roof' of climbers is ideal. If you use deciduous plants for screening purposes, you will allow welcome extra light to reach the patio in winter, when your need for privacy is not likely to be such a high priority.

Solid walls and fences do give privacy, but they block out light and sun. The best solution is usually to arrange a screen of plants, such as climbers trained over a trellis, which will help to give a little seclusion and which will cast only light, dappled shade.

TOO LITTLE TIME

You may feel that you work such long hours that, even if you have a patio garden, you will not have the time to make much use of it. Remember that a busy and tiring working life makes it even more important that you have an attractive, peaceful place to relax in your leisure hours. Plan your patio so that it can be used well into the evening – the garden can be a magical place after dark. Position it so that it is adjacent to the main living rooms for easy access, install efficient garden lighting and choose good quality garden furniture that will encourage you to eat and relax out of doors. Select plants that come into their own in the evening. White-flowered plants are particularly attractive in the twilight, and many flowers, including night-scented stock (*Matthiola bicornis*) and the tobacco plant (*Nicotiana* spp.), are at their most fragrant after dusk.

AN UNATTRACTIVE EXISTING PATIO

If you move into a house where the existing patio is dirty and unappealing, you do not have to replace it. Hire a power washer, which will make an incredible difference to the look of grimy paving. There are a number of products that will help you deal with the more difficult stains, but if the existing paving or concrete is beyond restoration, it is possible to lay a new surface directly on top of it, so that you do not have all the hard work of breaking it up. Make sure that the new surface is at least 15cm (6in) below the damp-proof course of any adjoining building. If you are in doubt, seek professional help.

PLANNING THE PATIO GARDEN

A patio garden may be constructed entirely from scratch or an existing patio area may be improved and converted. To avoid making expensive mistakes, it is worth taking plenty of time and care over the initial planning stage. Mistakes made in the early stages are the most difficult to correct and can never satisfactorily be disguised. The planning stage is, perhaps, the most important part of the entire scheme.

The first step is to take a notebook and write down everything you want from your patio garden. Your priority may be to have somewhere you can relax and entertain. You may want to have somewhere to grow choice, tender plants. Your ambition may be to add a feature that will enhance the appearance of your home. Writing down your priorities will help you to crystallize your thoughts and make clear the aspects that are important to you.

The next step is to take your notebook outside for a hard look at what you already have. Ask yourself why the existing space does not meet your needs. How could it be improved? What are its good and bad points? Is there anything you want to retain? Gradually, you will begin to get some idea of how easily the two lists — 'wants' and 'haves' — can be combined.

If you do not have an existing patio or patio garden there are all sorts of possibilities open to you. Before you make any firm decisions, take a closer look at your requirements, especially in terms of position and size.

POSITION

If you have a choice of site for the patio you will want to select the most suitable one, of course, but your decision will have to take several factors into account. Constructing the patio so that it is adjacent to the house is convenient and will allow the garden to be used more frequently and without special effort. It is also easy for services such as water and electricity. However, a position next to the house may not be the ideal site. Ask yourself if the area receives full sun and, if so, at what time of the day. Does that fit in with the times you are most likely to want to use the patio? Do you necessarily want a site in full sun? Perhaps a position that would be pleasantly shady during the hottest months of the year but bright in winter, when a low-lying sun is able to reach it, would suit you better than one that

is in full summer sun but gloomy in winter.

Privacy is usually a consideration. Is the area

ABOVE By placing a seating area in light shade, you can sit and enjoy the garden on the hottest of summer days.

near the house overlooked by neighbouring properties? It is usually possible to screen a patio garden, but a position some way from the house might offer greater privacy and may have a better outlook. Overhanging trees could also be a problem. Falling leaves will have to be cleared away in autumn, and some trees, such as limes (Tilia spp.), drip sticky honeydew onto paving and furniture. Your own trees can be thinned or removed, but persuading a neighbour to prune may be more difficult.

SIZE

It can be difficult to get the right balance – you want an area that is small enough to be intimate but large enough to be useful. The usual recommended size for a patio is to allow 3.3 square metres (4 square yards) for each member of the household. This may be a useful starting point for your calculations, but in a patio garden plants are important, so you should allow extra space for them. Remember, too, that the area will always look smaller when it is filled with pots, plants, furniture and so on.

If you intend to use paving slabs to cover the patio, make sure that the overall size and shape of the patio is in units of the slabs so that you do not have to cut more slabs than neccessary to fit.

CONVERTING AN EXISTING PATIO

Having the bare bones of a patio garden in existence can be a great help, saving both expense and the disruption of construction work. It could, however, also be a disadvantage, a straitjacket that will stifle creativity and prevent you from ever achieving the patio garden you really want. Sometimes it is best simply to abandon what is there and to begin all over again.

Have a close look at the hard surface. Is it reasonably attractive or is it an eyesore? The appearance may be greatly improved by thorough cleaning with a pressure sprayer, or you may be able to disguise an unattractive surface with containers and ornaments, but such solutions are never entirely satisfactory. If the surface is damaged or breaking up it is sometimes possible to make spot repairs

ABOVE *City dwellers often make privacy their number one planning priority. Trellising and* *fast-growing ivy are two of the most useful elements in the designer's lexicon.*

or to turn damaged areas into planting beds, but such damage is likely to be an indication of poor preparation in the first place and the condition of the patio will probably continue to deteriorate.

If the existing surface is not satisfactory, find out how easy it will be to replace it. Sometimes old slabs can be lifted easily, but if they have been bedded on cement it is a different matter. Concrete surfaces may, if they are thin, be fairly easy to break up, but a deep layer of concrete will be extremely difficult to dig up. If the existing surface is level and has been laid on a well-prepared base, new paving can often be laid directly on top, saving a lot of labour and expense. Check the position of the damp-proof course in any adjacent walls before you begin. If you are in doubt about any of the construction work needed, it is always best to consult an expert.

DRAWING UP A PLAN

✤ Whether you are starting afresh or improving an existing feature, always make a scale drawing of your proposed scheme. It does not need to be artistic, but try to make it accurate and use graph paper. Add the positions of important structural features such as pools *(see pages 60–61)* and raised beds *(see pages 56–57)* to make sure there is enough available space. Walls and fences should also be shown, as should the position of mains supplies, such as water and gas. Once you are satisfied that the plan is workable, choose the materials and start the preparations.

A SHADY BACKYARD

Gardens that are entirely enclosed by high walls have the benefit of shelter and seclusion, but on the minus side they are also very often shaded. Low light levels make the area difficult for plant growth; it could also appear dim and unwelcoming for people. It is important to choose shade-tolerant plants, which will thrive in the conditions; plants that need sunshine will soon look spindly and sickly, giving the whole garden a depressing atmosphere. (A list of plants that tolerate shady conditions can be found on page 21.)

With this courtyard, care has been taken to position the main planting opposite the window of the house, where it can be enjoyed from indoors. This means that the garden can still be appreciated in winter, when the weather might make it difficult or undesirable to get out into the garden. Shrubs and a well-positioned container help to disguise a utilitarian shed, and a statue forms a focal point for year-round interest.

Because the courtyard is secluded and sheltered, it will be an appealing place to sit out and enjoy a meal or a cup of coffee, despite the lack of direct sun; a table and chairs are situated so that they too overlook the main area of planting. Garden furniture comes in a variety of materials, from wood to wrought iron, but choose good quality tables and chairs that will withstand all weathers, as it can become tedious bringing furniture indoors night after night.

Temporary seasonal colour is provided by the range of pots grouped around the courtyard, which can be planted up with bulbs for spring, then followed by a succession of bedding plants. Alternatively, a range of shrubs may be selected. To maximize the available light, use light-coloured materials, or paint brick walls white or a light colour (though the warm shade of natural brick can be valuable).

LIGHTING IN THE GARDEN

This courtyard would be an ideal candidate for the use of artificial lighting to bring it alive at night, when shade is no longer a consideration. Because of its sheltered situation and proximity to the house, it is likely to be very suitable for use after dark. There is a wide range of lighting options for a patio garden, some of which are described on pages 40–41. Lighting can also be used in and around water, although a qualified electrician must be hired to do the job when the 240-volt supply from the house is going to be run out to the garden. The electrician will install a transformer and a circuit breaker which will allow a much safer 12-volt lighting system to be used in the garden.

> ### HINTS AND TIPS
>
> ❧ Use light-coloured building materials and accessories, because these reflect the maximum amount of light.
> ❧ Do not overcrowd a shaded garden with plants, as this can make the area even gloomier. A few choice plants can be much more effective than a cluster of unremarkable species dominating a patio.

BELOW *By removing a few slabs from the patio surface, planting pockets can be created. This foxglove corner adds height and interest to a bare wall.*

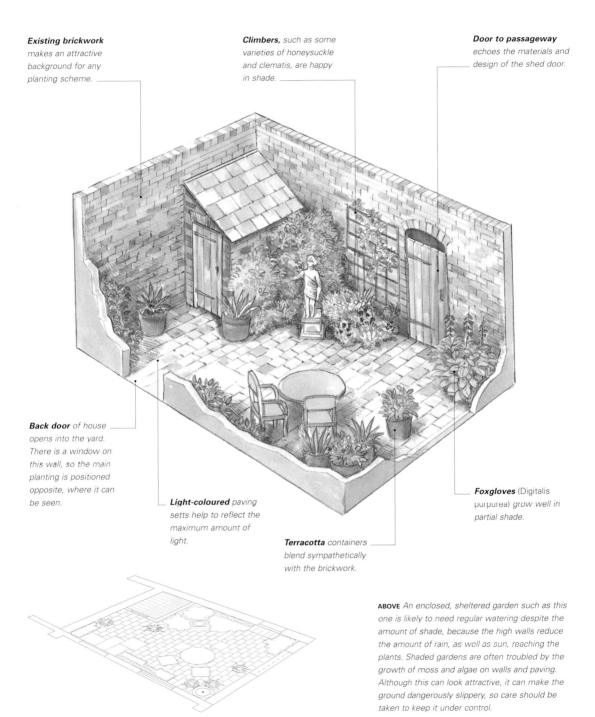

Existing brickwork makes an attractive background for any planting scheme.

Climbers, such as some varieties of honeysuckle and clematis, are happy in shade.

Door to passageway echoes the materials and design of the shed door.

Back door of house opens into the yard. There is a window on this wall, so the main planting is positioned opposite, where it can be seen.

Light-coloured paving setts help to reflect the maximum amount of light.

Terracotta containers blend sympathetically with the brickwork.

Foxgloves (Digitalis purpurea) grow well in partial shade.

ABOVE An enclosed, sheltered garden such as this one is likely to need regular watering despite the amount of shade, because the high walls reduce the amount of rain, as well as sun, reaching the plants. Shaded gardens are often troubled by the growth of moss and algae on walls and paving. Although this can look attractive, it can make the ground dangerously slippery, so care should be taken to keep it under control.

GARDEN WITH RAISED BEDS

This is a garden for those who want an attractive retreat but do not have a lot of time to spend weeding, watering and carrying out other routine tasks. The surfaces are easy to keep clean, and provide an ideal arena for entertaining – there is plenty of open space to accommodate people, and both the wide steps and the walls of the raised beds provide extra seating, should this be needed. The built-in barbecue is likely to receive plenty of use on summer evenings from all members of the family!

Although this is a low-maintenance, easily maintained garden, it nevertheless has plenty of points of interest. The York stone paving is easy to look after, requiring only occasional sweeping; although there is a large area of paving, it is prevented from being overpowering by some contrasting brick detail and a number of changes in level. Shallow steps leading down to the circular paved area make this a focal point, and an ideal location for hosting a dinner party on a pleasant summer's evening.

POINTS TO CONSIDER

🍃 Be realistic about the amount of time that you can spend on the garden. If you would rather spend your free time entertaining than gardening, plan your garden accordingly.

🍃 A large area of paving can look very harsh and stark – make sure that you plan some features that will break up and soften its appearance.

WHERE TO PLANT

Raised beds are quicker and easier to care for than beds situated at ground level. These have been planted up with easy-care shrubs and evergreen ground-cover plants, to reduce the amount of maintenance needed to a minimum. A step-by-step guide to making a raised bed can be found on pages 56–57.

Containers have several uses in this garden. Some are planted with permanent features, such as elegant mophead trees and spiky architectural plants; others are filled with annual bedding to provide a splash of spring, summer or autumn colour. Containers are a particularly convenient choice for busy gardeners, as varying numbers can be planted up according to the time available: these can then be treated as 'optional extras' in a labour-saving garden such as this one. (However, you should bear in mind that watering many containers can be time consuming.)

Pots of herbs are always an attractive, scented feature: here, they are positioned just outside the back door which makes it particularly convenient for the cook to nip out and gather a bunch of herbs to add to the pot during cooking.

LEFT *Raised beds are ideal for busy gardeners or for people who have restricted mobility. This corner bed is filled with hostas and shrub roses.*

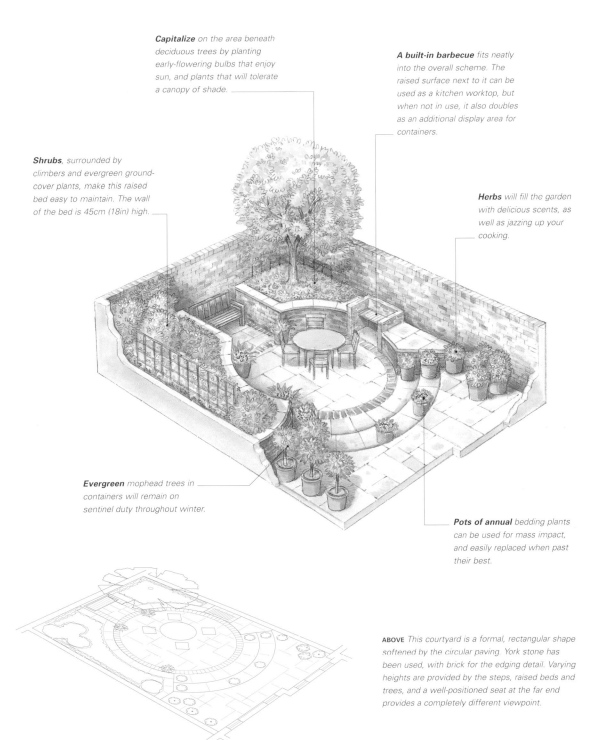

Capitalize on the area beneath deciduous trees by planting early-flowering bulbs that enjoy sun, and plants that will tolerate a canopy of shade.

A built-in barbecue fits neatly into the overall scheme. The raised surface next to it can be used as a kitchen worktop, but when not in use, it also doubles as an additional display area for containers.

Shrubs, surrounded by climbers and evergreen ground-cover plants, make this raised bed easy to maintain. The wall of the bed is 45cm (18in) high.

Herbs will fill the garden with delicious scents, as well as jazzing up your cooking.

Evergreen mophead trees in containers will remain on sentinel duty throughout winter.

Pots of annual bedding plants can be used for mass impact, and easily replaced when past their best.

ABOVE This courtyard is a formal, rectangular shape softened by the circular paving. York stone has been used, with brick for the edging detail. Varying heights are provided by the steps, raised beds and trees, and a well-positioned seat at the far end provides a completely different viewpoint.

ENCLOSED CENTRAL COURTYARD

*T*his type of garden is in the most traditional courtyard style — entirely surrounded by the dwelling. It would be unusual to find a single private house with such a central atrium now, but it is becoming more common as a feature of housing complexes, where the houses on each side belong to different owners. In many cases there is access to the garden from each house, making it a communal feature.

A major feature of this courtyard is the strongly patterned brick floor, laid in a basket-weave design. Since the brick extends over the entire surface, all the planting is confined to containers. This does not mean that planting has to be predictable or unimaginative. The type and style of containers used are varied, to bring added interest to the garden. A hanging basket and a decorative urn raised on a plinth help to give height to what could otherwise easily become a rather one-dimensional arrangement. Using containers made of different materials, or finished in unusual glazes, is another way of preventing monotony.

Plant extra-special speci-mens in large, striking containers to produce a stunning focal point for this enclosed garden.

BELOW *If your garden relies heavily on containers, select a range of plants with different seasons of interest, together with evergreens for structure.*

Seating has been provided in various areas of the garden so that differing perspectives can be enjoyed, and there is also plenty of room for a table and chairs. The traditional wood of the garden bench harmonizes with the table and surrounding chairs.

In keeping with the traditional air of this courtyard, there is a water feature with moving water to provide life and interest, and a satisfying splash to please the ear. A selection of water features for you to consider is provided on pages 34–35 and 60–61.

SELECTING PLANTS

A completely enclosed garden such as this one would be likely to have a considerable amount of shade cast by the surrounding buildings, and appropriate plants would need to be chosen with care. A selection of plants that will tolerate shade appears on page 21.

The only access to this type of garden is through the house, which makes frequent replanting of containers a little more awkward. With this in mind, it is better to choose shrubs, perennials and alpines as container plants, which do not need replacing every year like annuals and bedding. Before purchasing plants, check whether they will grow successfully in containers.

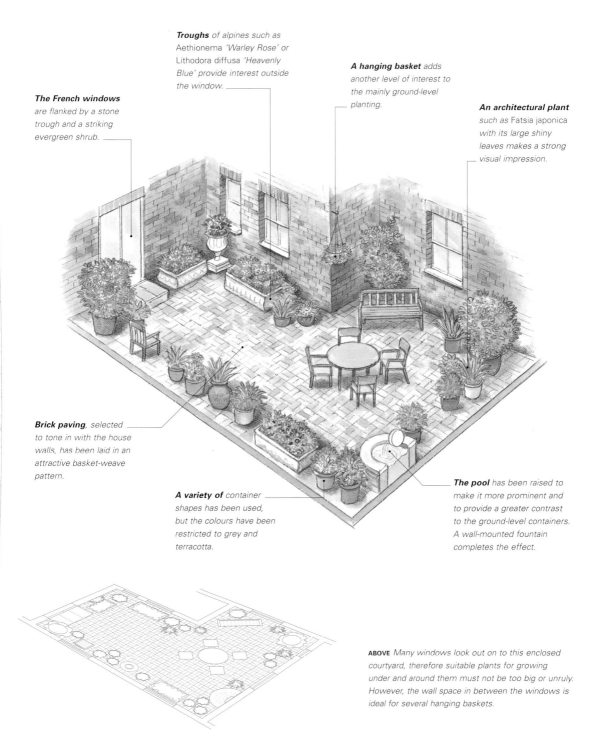

Troughs of alpines such as Aethionema 'Warley Rose' or Lithodora diffusa 'Heavenly Blue' provide interest outside the window.

A hanging basket adds another level of interest to the mainly ground-level planting.

The French windows are flanked by a stone trough and a striking evergreen shrub.

An architectural plant such as Fatsia japonica with its large shiny leaves makes a strong visual impression.

Brick paving, selected to tone in with the house walls, has been laid in an attractive basket-weave pattern.

A variety of container shapes has been used, but the colours have been restricted to grey and terracotta.

The pool has been raised to make it more prominent and to provide a greater contrast to the ground-level containers. A wall-mounted fountain completes the effect.

ABOVE Many windows look out on to this enclosed courtyard, therefore suitable plants for growing under and around them must not be too big or unruly. However, the wall space in between the windows is ideal for several hanging baskets.

29

CREATING YOUR GARDEN

2

O nce you have decided on the basic plan for your patio garden it is time to put it all into practice. The following pages tell you all you need to know about building and creating your garden, from choosing and laying the surface to building features such as raised beds and water gardens, and adding the finishing touches such as lighting and containers. There is also advice on choosing and buying plants for containers and beds, and ensuring they thrive.

LEFT *Dramatic colour contrasts turn a plain wall into an artist's canvas of rich hues, shapes and textures.*

CHOOSING THE MATERIALS · CHOICES

 ①

GRAVEL AND COBBLES

Gravel has much to recommend it, not least that it is easily obtainable, cheap and easy to lay. It has a pleasant, natural appearance, suitable for formal and informal settings, and it can be used in a variety of shapes, both geometric and naturalistically curved. Available in a range of colours, textures and sizes, you can use it to create the effect you want.

Cobbles look especially appropriate in a courtyard garden. They are, however, very time consuming to lay. They must be bedded in mortar, which itself should be contained within an edging of bricks or concrete strips. Cobbles can, however, look wonderful when they are used to create patterns with another material or to mark an edge, and they are useful for filling in awkward corners.

CHOICE CHECKLIST

∾ Make patterns with gravel in contrasting colours.
∾ Cobbles are difficult to walk on and should not be used on areas that receive a lot of pedestrian traffic.

∾ Rounded pea gravel has the most decorative appearance, but is more expensive and harder to obtain than ordinary gravel.

 ②

CONCRETE PAVING SLABS AND SETTS

Perhaps the most popular patio surface of all, concrete paving slabs are available in a wide range of sizes, shapes, colours and finishes and in a range of prices. Slabs should be laid on mortar on a thoroughly prepared base. Altering a patio laid with concrete paving slabs will be difficult.

Granite setts are cut from hard granite. They are extremely attractive, if expensive, and can stand up to a lot of hard wear. Before you choose granite setts, think about the wider environment of your garden: grey granite will look out of place in areas where the stone does not occur naturally. In the right place, however, granite setts will create a natural-looking surface, which will provide a sympathetic background for plants of all kinds.

CHOICE CHECKLIST

∾ Attractive patterns can be created by using slabs in two contrasting colours.
∾ Mix up to three different sizes of slab for a natural-looking, rustic effect.

∾ Paving slabs are available in a variety of different finishes. Choose a rough surface to give a safe grip.

 ❸

STONE PAVING, BRICKS AND PAVIORS

Formally cut natural stone, such as York stone, is the perfect choice for a formal garden and, although expensive, is one of the most aesthetically pleasing of all hard surfaces and will last a lifetime.

Water- and frost-proof bricks are a hardwearing and attractive option, available in a wide range of textures, colours and styles, and they can be laid in a variety of patterns, from herringbone to basket-weave.

Like bricks, paviors are relatively small, and are available in a range of shapes, colours and textures. Clay paviors are made in shades of red, while concrete paviors are usually grey or buff coloured. They are extremely attractive and are suitable for awkward shapes and corners.

CHOICE CHECKLIST

∾ Remember that not all bricks are suitable for paving.
∾ Natural stone is slippery when wet, which may be a consideration if elderly people use the garden.

∾ Ensure that natural stone has not been removed from an environmentally endangered source.

 ❹

TILES AND TIMBER DECKING

Tiles are suitable for more formal areas. Quarry tiles are made of fired clay, and they have a warm, rather rustic appearance, whereas ceramic tiles, which may be glazed and brightly coloured, are especially suitable for areas that are treated as 'outdoor rooms'. There is a wide range of colours, textures and sizes. Most need to be grouted, so the choice of a suitable grouting material is key to achieving a harmonious and pleasing effect.

Timber decking is an increasingly popular choice for patios. It has a warm, natural appearance and creates a link between the garden and indoors. Wood is especially suitable next to a smaller property, where a stone construction might appear to be too dominant and out of proportion.

CHOICE CHECKLIST

∾ Check that the tiles are frost-proof before you buy.
∾ In wet climates pressure-treated timber must be used.

∾ Timber decking requires special supporting structures, and in some areas there are building regulations to observe. Seek specialist help if you are in any doubt.

WATER IN THE PATIO GARDEN • CHOICES

 ❶

CONTAINER POOL

This type of pool is the easiest way to introduce the pleasures of water into even the smallest patio area. The most popular container is a wooden half-barrel, but any leak-proof container of a suitable size can be used. If the container is wood, coat the interior with bitumen paint to make sure it is waterproof. It will usually hold one or two gold-fish, a waterlily and three or four other pond plants, but it is important to choose miniature varieties.

Waterlilies such as the yellow-flowered *Nymphaea* x *helvola* are good choices for a small container, as is the double-flowered marsh marigold (*Caltha palustris* 'Flore Pleno'). Remember to include some oxygenating plants which will help to keep the water clear.

 ❷

SUNKEN AND RAISED POOLS

On a patio, a formal square, round or rectangular pool is often the most appropriate. Because small pools are harder to keep clean than larger ones, a patio pool should be as large as practicable to prevent it from freezing in winter and becoming overheated and filled with algae in summer.

Raised pools are perhaps the most attractive solution in a patio garden, but they are also demanding in terms of construction. The supporting walls must be strong and well built to withstand the pressure on them. Most raised pools are partly sunk, with only a proportion of the depth above ground level. Even these types of raised pool are more prone than their sunken equivalent to damage from extremes of temperature.

CHOICE CHECKLIST

∾ Plants should be set in loam-based compost topped with a good layer of gravel in special pond planting crates.

∾ Small pools are subject to damage by extremes of temperature, so site them carefully and, in cold climates, move fish to a tank indoors for the winter.

CHOICE CHECKLIST

∾ Set plants in planting crates rather than directly in soil on the base of the pool.
∾ Choose a good selection of oxygenators, deep water and marginal plants.

∾ Any paving surrounding the pool should overlap the edge to protect the butyl liner from direct sunlight.

WATER WITHOUT A POOL

A permanent pool of standing water can be a hazard in gardens where there are young children. It is much safer to install features in which a spout provides a sparkling jet of water that catches the light in the most pleasing fashion. This jet may originate from wall-mounted masks, containers of pebbles, millstones, urns or any of the numerous decorative ornaments that are available, especially from specialist water garden suppliers. The falling water drains through pebbles or gravel laid on a fine wire mesh to a sump below ground and is constantly re-circulated by a pump. This type of water feature is especially appropriate in gardens where children play since the water's surface is not accessible to them.

CHOICE CHECKLIST

❧ A self-contained water feature can be obtained as a complete, ready-to-install kit from many suppliers.

❧ Pebbles or stones that are part of a water feature and are kept constantly wet will need regular cleaning and drying to prevent excessive algae growth.

FOUNTAINS AND WATERFALLS

Much of the attraction of water is provided by its movement, with the soft, tinkling splash to please the ear and the glittering sparkle to catch the eye. A small electric pump (or even a solar panel) can be used to power a fountain or water spout.

A submersible pump is the simplest type to use. A fountain helps to aerate the pool and keep the water fresh. However, the flowers of waterlilies soon decay under a constant rain of droplets.

Waterfalls are less common than fountains and may well require more room than you have available in your patio garden. They can however be introduced on a fairly small scale if you have two pools on different levels. The water must fall directly over the lip to give a satisfactory splash.

CHOICE CHECKLIST

❧ Fountain kits usually provide a selection of interchangeable spray heads.
❧ Always seek specialist advice when using electricity with water.

❧ Both fountains and waterfalls can be useful to aerate the pool. This can help keep fish alive during thunderstorms and humid weather.

CONTAINERS • CHOICES

POTS, TUBS, BARRELS AND CASKS

These may be round, square, octagonal or a number of fancy shapes, including urns and wine jars. All types of plants can be grown in them, and the larger tubs are even suitable for larger perennial plants such as trees and shrubs.

Wooden barrels and casks are versatile containers and will impart a rustic flavour to almost any garden. They can be used to grow a variety of plants, from bedding plants to fruit and vegetables. Large barrels make ideal homes for strawberries, while smaller vessels are the perfect host for summer plants such as marigolds and alyssum. Traditionally made from oak, these containers have also been fashioned from chestnut, spruce, beech and elm.

CHOICE CHECKLIST

∾ Stand wooden tubs on three bricks to raise them off the ground; this ensures adequate drainage. Allowing plants to stand in water can cause considerable damage.

∾ Water-retentive crystals can be added to the potting compost in containers to prevent it drying out too quickly, though they will still need regular watering.

WINDOWBOXES

Windowboxes are rectangular troughs intended for use immediately outside a window – either suspended below, or standing on, a window ledge. As well as making the outside of the house look attractive, their plant displays can be enjoyed from inside the house, too. When they are used on houses with casement windows, they are usually best mounted on brackets below the window ledge, so they do not impede the opening of the windows.

Windowboxes can be used very successfully where a house wall forms part of the patio garden, helping the house integrate with the wider garden design. They can also be used on sheds or other outbuildings surrounding the patio area, as well as on plain walls.

CHOICE CHECKLIST

∾ Windowboxes must be supported so that they do not fall to the ground. You would be liable for any injury caused by an inadequately supported container.

∾ Drainage trays are useful, but make sure that boxes are not left standing in water for days on end.

Hanging baskets

Hanging baskets are ideal for small garden areas, because they make use of what would otherwise be 'dead' space, and they help to bring a three-dimensional aspect to the patio garden. There are several variations on the traditional wirework design. Solid-sided baskets (which are really suspended pots) have become popular because they dry out less quickly, but they cannot be planted to give the same 'all-round' effect as a traditional basket.

Brackets to hold baskets can be mounted on walls, pillars and posts, or they can also be suspended from the overhead beams of pergolas. Even at a low level, baskets can make an attractive feature and are certainly easier to care for.

CHOICE CHECKLIST

✎ A fully planted hanging basket is heavy so make sure the bracket is securely fixed.
✎ Self-watering baskets reduce the amount of watering to be done.

✎ Wire baskets with wide gaps between the wires are much easier to plant up than baskets that are fitted with a close mesh.

Wheelbarrows

Wheelbarrows make wonderful containers for patio gardens. An old wheelbarrow, no longer fit for service, can be quite literally put out to seed. Standing sedately in the middle of a lawn or patio, overrun by an abundance of plants, it appears to have graciously admitted defeat and become part of the garden itself. Either metal or wooden wheelbarrows can be used, but metal does not seem to have quite the same charm as wood, and also lacks its important insulating properties.

Plant a couple of larger plants in the centre, with a collar of cascading and trailing types around the edges. You could consider painting a wheelbarrow in soft pastel shades, but remember to choose flowers that blend in with their container.

CHOICE CHECKLIST

✎ A wooden wheelbarrow should be lined with plastic or the interior painted with bitumen-based paint to stop the wood rotting.

✎ If you cannot find a genuine old wooden wheelbarrow, garden centres sell ornamental ones, though they are on the small side. Avoid modern wheelbarrows.

BEDS AND BORDERS • CHOICES

①

PLANTING IN CRACKS

For an informal effect, low-growing, spreading plants can be set in cracks and crevices between paving slabs or in crazy paving (keep them out of the way of paths and walkways). A long-bladed knife is useful for scraping out and enlarging the crevice, and some good quality soil or compost can be trickled into the hole to get the plants away to a good start. Single small paving slabs or individual stones from a crazy paving can be removed to give a slightly larger planting hole.

Remove the plant from its pot and crumble or wash away some of the compost from around the roots to enable it to be tucked into the prepared planting hole. Trickle a little more soil around it and firm it into place.

CHOICE CHECKLIST	
❧ Hummocks of plants dotted about the surface can be a hazard to anyone walking through the area.	❧ Some plants spread further than required, occasionally even lifting paving slabs, leaving an uneven and potentially dangerous surface.

②

CREATING A SMALL BED

If you are working with an existing patio or forgot to include possibilities for low-level planting in your original scheme, you may find that you can remove some of the patio's surface to give more planting space. This process is possible only if the paving has been laid directly on a firm bed without mortar, because one or more slabs can then simply be levered up, giving you access to the soil.

A pattern of small beds can be created by removing slabs at various points within the patio. The soil exposed should be well dug and replaced if it is of poor quality, with some slow-release fertilizer incorporated into the new compost. If you have a gravelled area, you will find that many low-growing plants establish themselves very quickly.

CHOICE CHECKLIST	
❧ Plant a mixture of low-growing alpines or several plants of the same type to form a solid block of colour.	❧ If the gravel lies on a weed-preventing membrane, cut through so that the plant's roots can be inserted into the underlying soil.

3

SPECIMEN PLANTS

A large, architectural plant growing in the soil through the patio's surface can form a striking focal point for the patio garden. This is a good way to grow a small tree, because it will be able to develop more fully than it would in a container.

It is possible to buy paving material that is designed with this type of planting in mind – for example some slabs have a segment removed from one corner. When you are using this type of paving, prepare the planting area and complete the planting before laying the paving around it. If the surface is made from other types of paving, slabs can be lifted in the same way as for a small bed, but lift them over a larger area to enable you to prepare the ground more thoroughly.

CHOICE CHECKLIST

❧ If you have a patio surface laid on a bed of concrete you should confine the planting to raised beds and containers.

❧ Remember to provide a tree or tall plant with a suitable stake, as it will be difficult to add one afterwards.

4

RAISED BEDS

Raised beds require more construction work, but they have a number of advantages over traditional beds. Where it is impossible to break up the surface of the patio, raised beds can simply be built on top of it. They add a valuable visual element of three-dimensionality to the patio garden, and their height makes them easier to maintain than beds at ground level, which is an important factor if the garden is kept by someone who is elderly or whose mobility is impaired. In a reasonably sized patio or court-yard garden, a mixture of raised and ground-level beds with complementary planting looks very effective. And because raised beds bring plants up to the level of the gardener, it is also easier to admire and enjoy them.

CHOICE CHECKLIST

❧ Raised beds can allow you to grow plants that would not flourish in the soil in beds and borders.
❧ Height makes raised beds easier to maintain.

❧ The additional height cuts down on bending and stooping to admire specimen plants.

LIGHTING • CHOICES

FLARES, CANDLES AND LANTERNS

A living flame can create a wonderful atmosphere in a patio garden. The drawbacks are that it is relatively short-lived, requires care when lighting and when in use, and gives a very low intensity of light. Candles or night lights need to be protected from the wind or they will be forever blowing out. Glass containers are popular as they let maximum light through – coloured glass gives a range of pretty effects. Metal containers with a pattern of holes stamped in the sides produce a flickering fretwork of light when a candle burns inside.

Lanterns can be hung from branches or crook-necked stakes, but must be firmly fixed in a safe position. Another alternative is wax flares, which are pushed into the soil and will burn for hours.

CHOICE CHECKLIST

❧ Scented candles deter biting insects, which can often be a nuisance at night.
❧ No naked flame should be left unattended in the garden for any length of time.

❧ For safety, choose stable, broad-based containers, which are less likely to be knocked over.

ELECTRIC LIGHT

Electricity has the great bonus of convenience. It is very versatile, and can power lighting that is low and atmospheric or intensely bright. Security lighting uses very bright floodlighting, which is too harsh for general use. Lower intensity mains lighting can give a useful light for eating or sitting out on the patio after dark.

Solar-powered lights are one option for lighting the garden. The integral solar cell must be positioned so that it receives as much sunlight as possible during the day in order to give out a reasonable light at night. Solar-powered lights are most useful as marker lights for paths or entrances where only low-intensity light is required, but their lack of controllability can be annoying.

CHOICE CHECKLIST

❧ All mains lighting should be installed by a qualified electrician.

❧ Solar-powered light fades quite quickly, and in overcast weather there may be insufficient sunlight to charge the solar cell at all.

 LIGHTING EFFECTS

As well as lighting the sitting area on the patio, it is also possible to create interesting effects by lighting different parts of the garden that can be viewed from the patio. Choose a focal point such as a specimen shrub or a statue, and experiment with uplighting, downlighting and backlighting. Strong contrasts of light and shadow can produce dramatic effects.

Shaded lights produce a more gentle glow and are very effective when strategically placed among groups of garden plants. It may also be possible to incorporate lights into the surface material of the patio when you first lay it out by using reinforced glass or clear plastic panels through which the lights shine upwards.

CHOICE CHECKLIST

❧ Low voltage lighting systems are the safest to use in the garden, and kits are available for easy home installation. See pages 62–63 for more details.

❧ Consider access when siting lights as you will need to change light bulbs or clean glass shades.

 UNDERWATER LIGHTS

A water feature is always an excellent subject for lighting. In addition to spotlights positioned round the pool, specially designed lamps can also be submerged beneath the water. These may be fixed spotlights, which shine up through the water, or they may float freely on the pond's surface. Most are supplied with changeable coloured lenses for a range of different effects. Underwater lights are powered by electricity with the voltage reduced to a safe level through a transformer, which may need to be positioned under cover, though some transformers can be used under water.

Underwater spotlights are most effective when shining up into a fountain or cascade, where they highlight the moving water droplets.

CHOICE CHECKLIST

❧ Where there are fish in a pool, make sure that at least part of the pond remains in darkness at night to provide a safe retreat for them.

❧ Floating lights are best on a still pond, where their glow is reflected in the water's surface.

OBTAINING PLANTS

In many garden centres and in the catalogues of mail order plant suppliers you may find sections labelled 'patio plants'. The plants sold in this category are usually compact growers, which are suitable for containers, and they are colourful and showy and often rather exotic and unusual. There are, however, no hard and fast rules to say what makes a plant suitable for a patio garden, and the range of possibilities is vast and exciting.

Plants in containers probably form the mainstay of any patio garden, but there are plenty of other options. Where there is even a small amount of soil under the patio surface, some plants can make use of it. Creeping, mat-forming specimens set in gaps between paving slabs help to soften a large expanse of hard surface, and climbers planted at the base of walls enable the vertical dimensions of the garden to be brought to life. These plants often bring the bonus of fragrance into your garden. Raised beds provide a larger volume of compost for plants that would find smaller containers too restricting, and the retaining walls are the perfect home for many charming alpines, which can be tucked in the crevices of the stonework.

There are, obviously, some plants that are simply not suitable for the patio garden. Very tall, spreading or vigorously growing trees and shrubs would soon be out of scale, although they can, if you wish, be grown as short-term plants, which you discard once they start to become too large. Plants with only a brief season of interest do not usually earn their place in a garden where, because of its small size, they are on show at all times. Very prickly plants can be a nuisance where people are likely to be brushing past them frequently, and if small children use the patio garden, you may want to think twice about including poisonous plants, such as oleander and brugmansia.

OBTAINING PLANTS

When you are planting up a new patio garden for the first time, trees, shrubs and herbaceous perennials are likely to be required as 'one-off' purchases to form the permanent backbone of the design. In addition to these, a range of bedding plants and tender perennials, which will be replaced every year, will provide a bright display of colour for the summer season.

Plants can be bought in from a number of suppliers, and, if you have suitable facilities, you can also raise some of your own plants from seed and cuttings. This is not only enjoyable and satisfying, but it can save quite a lot of money, because buying sufficient trays of bedding plants to fill several tubs, windowboxes and hanging baskets can easily cost as much as the containers themselves.

The ideal place in which to raise plants is a greenhouse, which should be heated sufficiently to keep it frost free. Seeds are sown in early spring, and the seedlings pricked out into trays or individual pots to grow on ready for planting out in mid- to late spring, after the last frosts. Seedlings must be hardened off gradually (accustomed to exterior conditions) before they are planted in their final positions outside. Increase numbers of existing plants by taking soft tip cuttings in spring from stock plants that have been overwintered, or take cuttings in late summer and overwinter them in a frost-free place for planting out in the following spring.

LEFT *Shopping for plants is one of the most pleasurable parts of creating a garden.*

BUYING PLANTS

There are four main sources of plants: garden centres, nurseries, non-specialist retailers and mail order.

Garden centres generally carry a good range of all types of plant, which are usually bought in from a variety of commercial growers. Most are container grown, which means they can be planted at any time of year. When you buy from nurseries, you may find that the stock has been grown on site, and trees and shrubs may be lifted from open ground to be planted in the dormant season.

Inspect the plants carefully before you buy, looking especially for potential pests and diseases – damage to the lower leaves may, for example, indicate the presence of vine weevils. Check the bottom of the pot to see whether a matted tangle of roots is protruding, as pot-bound plants sometimes never recover when transplanted.

Every spring, dozens of plants are available from a wide range of non-specialist outlets, including such diverse places as hardware stores, chain stores and local markets. The quality of the plants on offer can be variable, but the prices are often reasonable. Only the most popular varieties are stocked, however, so if you want something unusual, you will have to look elsewhere.

Many plants are available by mail order, including some rare specimens that are not readily available elsewhere. Specialist nurseries will despatch trees, shrubs and perennials in the dormant season, and huge numbers of bedding plants are sent out every spring. Carriage adds to the cost of the plants, but selling in bulk enables the prices to be kept competitive. When the plants arrive, unpack them immediately. Plants need light and water, and should remain in cardboard boxes for the shortest possible time.

HINTS AND TIPS

- Although container-grown plants can be planted all year round, spring and autumn are the most suitable times, and this is when you are likely to get the best quality and choice of plants at garden centres and nurseries.
- When buying mail order, choose an established, reputable company. Don't be afraid to return plants that are unsatisfactory when you receive them.
- Bare-root trees and shrubs should be planted immediately, or, if that is not possible, 'heeled in' temporarily to a spare piece of ground so that the roots are covered with soil and will not dry out.
- Always check the underside of a plant's leaves when looking for pests or diseases – this is often where the problem is first in evidence.

TECHNIQUE   SELECTING PLANTS IN CONTAINERS

1 The compost in the container must be moist but not waterlogged. If it is excessively wet, the roots may start to rot. Conversely, if dry they will also suffer.

2 If moss is present on the surface of the compost, this indicates that the plant has been neglected and has also been in the pot for too long.

3 Make sure that masses of roots are not protruding out of the container's drainage holes. This indicates that the plant is pot bound. Plants seldom fully recover if the roots are excessively matted.

4 Check that the plant has been grown in its container, and has not been recently potted up for a quick sale. Reputable suppliers will not try to mislead customers, and all plants should be clearly labelled.

WINDOWSILL PROPAGATION

A part from saving money, there is a wealth of satisfaction in successfully raising your own plants. Many plants suitable for patio gardens can be easily increased, including half-hardy annuals, shrubs and herbaceous perennials. If you have space, kitchen windowsills are the ideal place. Kitchens are usually warm, and it is easy to keep an eye on developing shoots. It is also very satisfying to watch them grow day by day.

Taking cuttings from softwood is a simple way of producing more plants. The term 'softwood' refers to the soft stem growth produced at the tip of a stem during the season of growth. Softwood has the highest capacity of all stems to produce roots. Although soft stem growth occurs naturally in the spring, it is possible to obtain softwood cuttings later in the season in high temperatures, which act as a catalyst to growth. Where pots may be kept on windowsills indoors or in sheltered nooks, softwood propagation is particularly appropriate. By pruning back the parent plant vigorously in winter, increasing the temperature and taking the cutting as soon as enough tip growth appears, rooting is more likely to occur.

SOWING PLANTS

The seeds of half-hardy annuals should be sown in gentle warmth (16–21°C/61–70°F) in greenhouses and conservatories in late winter or early spring. Once the seeds germinate, the young seedlings can be transferred to uniform spacings in a seed tray, where they are able to develop into healthy plants. They need to acclimatize slowly to outdoor conditions, and when all risk of frost has passed they can be planted into borders or containers.

An easy way to increase herbaceous perennials is to divide existing plants. This usually needs to be done every three or four years and is a task best tackled in early spring, although in mild areas autumn is also suitable. Find a congested clump, dig it up, and divide as shown below.

HINTS AND TIPS

🍂 Rooting powder is usually unnecessary for softwood cuttings, but brands with a fungicide can be helpful for slow-rooting subjects, to prevent rotting of the base of the cutting.
🍂 Always use sterile compost for sowing seeds in pots and trays and taking cuttings – garden soil contains too many potentially harmful micro-organisms for young plants.
🍂 Hardy annuals can often be sown outside, directly where they are to grow. Sow in short, straight rows so that they can be distinguished from weeds when they germinate.

TECHNIQUE   **DIVIDING HERBACEOUS PERENNIALS**

1 Carefully dig up a congested clump and place it on the border soil.

2 To divide the clump, insert two garden forks, back to back, in the clump's centre.

3 Lever the handles of the forks together to separate the entangled roots. Only when these are loose should you pull the forks out.

4 Pull plants apart, retaining only young pieces from around the edges. These then can be planted. Discard old parts from the plant's centre.

TECHNIQUE	SOWING HALF-HARDY ANNUALS

1 Fill a clean seed tray with compost and firm it down with your hand or a flat piece of wood. Water with a fine rose to moisten the compost evenly.

2 Tip the seeds into a piece of paper that has been folded to form a V-shape. Sprinkle evenly over the surface and then use a sieve to cover lightly with compost.

3 Place a transparent lid on top to conserve moisture and maintain a uniform temperature. Shade with a sheet of newspaper until the seedlings emerge.

TECHNIQUE	TAKING SOFTWOOD CUTTINGS

1 Take a softwood cutting early in the morning, when the stem will be retaining water. Select a shoot tip and cut off about 10cm (4in). Steps must be taken to avoid water loss, as this causes poor results.

2 Immediately put the cutting in a shady place, either sealed in a polythene bag, or in a bucket of water.

3 With a straight cut, trim the base of the stem just below a leaf joint. Remove the leaves from the bottom third of the stem. The cutting should now be about 5–7cm (2–3in) long.

4 Fill a flowerpot (or seed tray) with cuttings compost to within 1.25cm (½in) of the rim. Make a hole near the edge of the pot and insert a cutting, making sure the base of the stem is in firm contact with the compost. Plant three cuttings in each pot, making sure their leaves do not touch.

5 Water the cuttings, using a fine spray. To conserve moisture, cover with a polythene bag and secure with a rubber band. Ensure that the polythene does not touch the leaves. Spray the cuttings regularly with plain water.

6 Once the cuttings have rooted, in about two to three weeks, lift them carefully out of the pot and plant into individual pots. Use a compost such as John Innes No.1 or a similar mix. Harden off the cuttings by acclimatization before placing them outside.

KEEPING PLANTS HEALTHY

Plants must be watered, fed and pruned whether they are grown in the wider garden or in a patio or courtyard garden. Patio gardens are often sited close to the house, and their proximity may make it easier for you to keep an eye on your plants, removing dead leaves and dead-heading flowers as necessary, as well as allowing you to spot the first signs of any problems. It's easy to give a small area the attention it needs to keep it in tip-top condition.

During summer, container plants need to be watered about twice a day. Adding moisture-retentive materials to the compost in hanging baskets, as well as using moisture-retentive liners, helps to reduce the frequency of watering. Feeding and spraying must not be neglected, as a display can be ruined rapidly by an infestation of pests. Regularly feeding plants helps them to prosper and create an attractive display throughout summer.

GARDEN PESTS

Wherever plants are grown, there will be pests and diseases waiting to attack them. Sometimes the effects of these are very minor; at other times they can be devastating. Inspect plants regularly and look particularly closely at any that do not seem to be thriving. Pay special attention to the growing tips and the undersides of leaves, which is where problems may first show themselves. Make sure

the conditions you are providing are correct – it is easy to blame pests or diseases for symptoms that may be caused by bad growing techniques such as the wrong soil.

There are many pest and disease organisms that can attack plants, but relatively few are likely to cause any serious problems in the patio garden, and you would be very unfortunate indeed if you were to lose plants entirely.

Infestations of aphids can sometimes be washed off with a strong jet of water. There are many chemicals available including pirimicarb, which is specific to aphids.

Irregular holes chewed in leaves are often a sign of caterpillars. They have voracious appetites and can cause a great deal of damage. Large caterpillars can be hand picked and destroyed. Alternatively, use chemical treatments such as derris and bifenthrin.

Scale insects are sap-sucking pests that look like small limpets attached to stems and the undersides of leaves; they

---

HINTS AND TIPS

- Soil-less compost dries out more quickly than its soil-based equivalent, and is difficult to re-wet once dry. Adding moisture-retaining granules to the compost when you plant will help.
- Automatic watering systems are worth investigating if you have a collection of choice plants.
- Plants that are permanently grown in containers should be repotted into fresh compost in spring every year or two. When they are fully grown, top-dress by removing the top 5–8cm (2–3in) of compost and replacing this with new compost, mixed with some slow-release fertilizer.

TECHNIQUE — WATERING HANGING BASKETS

1 By tying a hosepipe to a cane, water can be gently trickled into a hanging basket. Proprietary fittings are available from garden centres, and these can be attached to hosepipes so windowboxes and hanging baskets can be watered easily.

2 If the compost in a hanging basket becomes very dry, take down the basket and stand it in a large bowl of water until bubbles cease to rise from the compost.

TECHNIQUE	FEEDING AND SPRAYING	WATCHPOINTS

1 Feed plants in containers regularly throughout summer, using a fertilizer dissolved in water. Apply this every ten to fourteen days. Always water the compost first, however, as applying fertilizer to dry compost will damage the roots of plants.

2 Because plants are packed together in containers, they provide convenient meals for pests. Inspect plants regularly and use an environmentally friendly spray that will not harm the atmosphere.

Patio gardens, which are generally built close to houses or, at least, near a garden wall, are often protected from the worst of cold weather by the proximity of buildings. Nevertheless, plants grown in containers are more susceptible to frost damage simply because their roots are above ground. If you do not have a greenhouse into which tender plants can be moved in winter, group containers together to afford some protection, and in exceptionally cold weather use horticultural fleece or plastic bubble wrap to protect precious plants.

exude a sticky honeydew on which sooty mould may grow. They are usually found on woody plants with leathery leaves, such as bay or oleander. They can be scraped off by hand if you have the patience. Scale insects are difficult to control with chemicals, but pirimiphos-methyl or malathion can be tried.

Although they prefer open beds, slugs and snails can still be a serious nuisance in the patio garden. Going out with a torch after dark to hunt them out and pick them off the plants can be productive, if rather unpleasant! Or try using organic controls, such as traps filled with beer. Beer is attractive to snails, who fall in the trap and drown. Chemical controls, such as metaldehyde and methiocarb, are poisonous to wildlife and should be used with caution.

Vine weevils are an increasingly common problem. They may attack any plant, but are especially fond of those grown in containers. The adult weevils eat notches out of foliage, but it is the larvae that cause the most problems. These white grubs live in the soil and eat plant roots, often escaping detection until the plant collapses and dies. A biological control is available in the form of a predatory nematode that attacks the larvae. Prevent the adults, that cannot fly, from crawling up the sides of containers by circling the container with a line of special non-set glue. Soil insecticides can be applied to the compost.

DISEASES

Powdery mildew is common on plants such as Michaelmas daisies, particularly if they are overcrowded. It is usually worse in hot, dry seasons when leaves and shoots become coated in a white powdery substance, which inhibits the plant's growth. Spray affected plants with a general fungicide such as carbendazim. Clear up and destroy all affected growth at the end of the season to prevent spores over-wintering.

Pale spots on the upper surface of leaves and concentric brown rings on the undersides indicate rust. Plants fail to thrive and lose their leaves early. Pelargoniums and antirrhinums are common candidates for rust disease. Remove and destroy affected leaves as soon as you notice them and then spray adjacent plants with a fungicide such as propiconazole.

Viruses cause a wide range of symptoms, from yellow mottling, streaking and mosaic patterns on the foliage to misshapen leaves or crinkled leaf edges. A wide range of plants may be affected, including buddleias, cyclamen, freesias, daffodils, pelargoniums and vines. Viruses are impossible to treat, and badly affected plants must be removed and destroyed. Many viruses are spread by aphids as they suck plants' sap, so keeping these pests under control is the best way to prevent the infection of plants.

PREPARING THE GROUND

Once you have chosen the site for a new patio garden, the area needs to be prepared for the construction work. Before you do anything else, establish where the positions of the water, electricity and gas mains are, because these may well run under the site. If you do not already know where they are, ask the relevant service supplier for the information. Mark the positions of the mains on the site and on your plan drawing, and remember to keep a copy of the scale plan in a safe place for future reference.

Clear the site of plants and turf. Encroaching tree roots can be a problem. It is usually best to avoid positioning a patio close to a large, established tree, not only because of the shade that will be cast in summer and the leaves that may fall in autumn, but because vigorous roots may disturb the paving. Bear in mind that your neighbour's boundary trees could pose the same problem.

Before you consider cutting back any tree roots, remember that root pruning must be carried out during a tree's dormant period and that it is often best to carry out any such pruning in two stages – making this a long-term solution. In the first year only prune the roots on one side of the tree, the following year, tackle the roots on the other side. Root pruning must be undertaken with care or it may well kill the tree, which may be what you want, of course. Never attempt to root prune your neighbour's tree – it is illegal to do so.

BUILDING WALLS

Building a wall to a height of about 1m (3ft) is within the capability of almost anyone with a basic knowledge of building techniques. However, if you are planning a wall over that height you should seek professional help. Not only are there structural problems to consider, including the provision of strengthening piers at regular intervals, but there may well be local planning restrictions on the construction of permanent barriers above a certain height.

If you are going to include a wall as part of your patio garden, the footings must be laid first.

PREPARING TO LAY THE SURFACE

Whatever type of surface you have chosen, it must be laid on a firm, level base, and this nearly always means excavating some of the existing soil and filling in with a layer of hardcore, which is then topped with sand to create a level

PROJECT	BUILDING A WALL

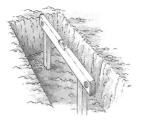

1 Dig a trench three times the proposed width of the wall and, for a wall no higher than 1m (3ft), make it at least 38cm (15in) deep. (This method is suitable for walls on chalky soil only.)

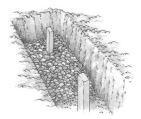

2 Consolidate the base, and then add a layer of hardcore to a depth of about 13cm (5in). Consolidate the hardcore.

3 Finally, add concrete to a depth of 15cm (6in). As a rough guide, in a trench that is 60cm (2ft) wide you will need about 150kg (330lb) of concrete for every metre (3ft). A wall that is built with a double row, with perhaps space for planting, will require proportionately deeper footings.

1 Make some levelling pegs about 30cm (12in) long from some 2.5 x 2.5cm (1 x 1in) timber. Measure 5cm (2in) down from one end of each peg and draw a line all the way round it. This is the level for the sand. If a layer of hardcore is needed, measure another 5cm (2in) down from the first line.

2 Mark out the area to be paved and dig out the loose topsoil to a sufficient depth to accommodate the foundation materials plus the depth of the surfacing material. Dig out an area that is slightly larger than the area to be paved, extending a few centimetres beyond each boundary.

3 Hammer a peg near a corner of the site. The top should sit below the surrounding soil by the depth of the paving, so the finished patio will be flush with the surrounding surface. Paving must be at least 15cm (6in) below the damp-proof course of the adjoining building.

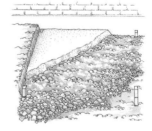

4 Continue to hammer pegs in straight lines at intervals of about 2m (6ft), keeping the lines parallel to the adjacent wall. Use a levelling board and a spirit level to keep the tops horizontal.

5 A paved surface must slope slightly to shed rainwater. Nail a 2.5cm (1in) block of wood to the underside of a 2m (6ft) levelling board. Use this board to place pegs in rows at right angles to the wall. The tops of the pegs will slope away from the house.

6 Fill the excavated site with hardcore, then sand, to the levels indicated on the levelling pegs. Tamp it down thoroughly. Use taut string, held on pegs, to mark the exact dimensions of the paved area. You are now ready to lay the surface.

bed on which the surface material can be laid. Because a patio garden only has to carry light, pedestrian traffic, the foundations do not have to be as deep as for, say, a drive that has to bear the weight of cars. The depth of foundations required for the patio will depend on the material to be laid. Small-unit paviors and bricks can be laid on a 5cm (2in) layer of sand spread on a firm soil base, but for paving slabs, there needs to be at least 10cm (4in) of hardcore below a 2.5cm (1in) layer of sand.

COVERING AN EXISTING SURFACE

If you decide to lay a new surface on top of an existing patio, sweep the surface thoroughly and make sure that rainwater drains away efficiently. Check that the finished, resurfaced patio will not be so high that it bridges a damp-proof course on the adjoining wall of the house, or that it covers an air brick. Ensure that the new surface is still 15cm (6in) away from the damp-proof membrane. Lay the new paving on a bed of mortar.

LAYING THE SURFACE

If your budget allows, a professional contractor should be able to lay your chosen surface competently and quickly. If possible, choose a contractor through personal recommendation, or, when you are obtaining estimates, ask to see examples of some recent work. Reputable contractors are usually only too willing to show off their best work.

Laying the surface for a small patio garden should not, however, be beyond the ability of any reasonably fit, active and handy homeowner. You will find it easier if there are two of you, but once the basic site preparation has been done *(see pages 48–49)*, laying the surface is usually relatively straightforward.

Whatever surface you intend to use, you should divide the area into manageable sections. Taut string, held on stakes driven securely into the ground, can be used not only to divide the area into equal sectors but also to guide you as you work. Always be realistic about the amount of work you are going to get done in a given time, particularly when working with concrete, which has to be used up quickly once it is mixed. Dividing the job up into smaller sections will allow you to take breaks as necessary.

WORKING WITH GRAVEL

Gravel can be obtained in bags from a garden centre or builders' merchant, or by the truckload direct from the quarry. Bagged gravel is more expensive but it tends to be easier to handle. Gravel from a truck is generally tipped

WATCHPOINTS

Manhole covers

Never concrete or pave over manhole covers. If the manhole cover is flush with the new surface, carefully positioned containers may be all that are required to disguise it. If a new surface, especially one laid over an existing patio, is above the level of the manhole cover, use a special metal container of the appropriate size to hold one or two paving stones, cut to size if necessary. The container and cover can be lifted clear if access for inspection is needed.

Mains supplies

When you are working in an area where there are service pipes or cables, take extra care when you are digging so that you do not damage them. If you uncover cables or pipes, fill in over them with fine soil, and bury a strip of marker tape about 8cm (3in) down along their path. All pipes, cables, stop cocks and so on must remain accessible once the patio surface is laid, and you may have to consider laying some slabs on a bed of sand rather than a solid concrete bed.

all on one spot, making it harder to spread evenly. It is important to use edging strips to hold the gravel in place otherwise it will spread sideways. The edging can be made from pressure-treated timber, bricks, paviors or concrete. Attractive patterns can be made by using contrasting colours of gravel. Gravel must have a firm base beneath it. About 5cm (2in) of scalpings or hoggin, compacted with a heavy roller or plate compactor, will be sufficient.

One disadvantage of gravel is that it tends to spread over adjacent surfaces and lawns, and it gets taken into the house on the soles of people's shoes. One way round this is to use resin-bonded gravel, where the stones are mixed with resin and the mixture is poured over the area to be covered and left to set. The finished appearance is similar to normal gravel although it has a glassy sheen which is not to everybody's taste.

PROJECT	GRAVEL

1 Put retaining edging strips of pressure-treated timber in place, held with pegs, before you lay gravel. Bricks set on edge should be anchored in mortar, as should tiles.

2 Lay gravel on a firm base of at least 5cm (2in) of compacted scalpings or hoggin. Do not lay more than about 2.5cm (1in) depth of gravel, or it will be difficult to walk on.

PROJECT COBBLES

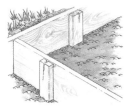

1 The cobbles are set into concrete. First, put shuttering in position to hold in the concrete. It is best to work in small sections, so that the concrete does not have a chance to harden too much before you insert the cobbles.

2 Prepare a base layer of 5cm (2in) compacted scalpings or sand and cover with a layer of concrete (1 part cement to 5 parts sharp sand). Aim to insert the cobbles so that 1–3cm (1in) protrudes above the surface of the concrete.

3 As soon as the concrete is in place and levelled, push the cobbles into it by hand, using a piece of board to keep their tops level.

4 Leave the concrete to set for a day or two, then brush a dry mix of 1 part cement to 3 parts sand between the cobbles. Spray with water to set the mortar and clean the stones.

PROJECT POURED CONCRETE

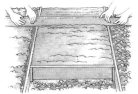

1 Sweep a layer of sand over the underlying layer of hardcore to make sure there are no gaps in it.

2 Divide the area to be concreted into sections no longer than 3m (10ft) long with planks which should be nailed to the levelling pegs, which are still in place *(see page 49)*.

3 Pour the prepared concrete into a section and make sure it reaches up to the edges and into the corners. Use a baulk of timber that stretches across the concrete to level the surface, working with a helper.

4 Because concrete expands it must be laid with breaks so that it does not crack. Lengths of timber should be used as temporary expansion joints; they can be removed when the concrete has set.

POURED CONCRETE

Concrete is normally used for fairly small areas of the garden, such as paths, rather than for large patio areas. Paving slabs are more popular because they are easier to lay, often cheaper, and more attractive. However, concrete makes a good hard-wearing surface which can be useful.

Concrete is a mixture of sand, cement and gravel. Once water is added it must be laid quickly before it starts to set, so it is vital not to mix more than you can handle at a time. You can mix it at home: small quantities can be mixed with a spade on a board, adding water from a watering can until a stiff mixture is obtained. For large quantities, cement mixers of various sizes can be hired. It is also possible to have ready-mixed concrete delivered, but you will need a team of assistants to enable you to spread the concrete before it goes off.

For maximum strength the concrete mix should be on the dry side and should be allowed to set slowly after laying. It is best if at all possible to avoid concreting if the weather is very hot or very cold as this will affect its setting.

SLABS, TILES AND PAVIORS

G*ravel and concrete surfaces are generally laid as a single block, all in one go. The most popular types of surfacing materials, however, come as smaller units — slabs, bricks, paviors and tiles among them. When laying this type of material, smaller sections can be tackled at a time — it is possible to spread the whole job over several days.*

When planning any area using paving slabs or small unit paving, try to estimate the quantities of materials required as accurately as you can. Err on the side of over- rather than under-ordering. If you run out of materials, work may be held up while you wait for a new delivery; materials from a different batch may also show a slight variation in their colour or finish. Although this is likely to be slight, it may be irritatingly noticeable in the finished surface. Remember to allow for breakages and spoiled slabs, particularly where the cutting of slabs or bricks is involved.

PLAYING SAFE

If you are not used to heavy manual work, take care when undertaking a job such as laying a patio surface. It is possible to hire equipment such as slab lifters and sack trolleys that make life easier for you and help to avoid the likelihood of back strain and damaged muscles. Work at a sensible pace; don't overdo things simply in order to get the job done in one weekend.

RIGHT *Small pots of flowers add a decorative touch to steps, but do not obstruct the path.*

PROJECT	PAVING SLABS

1 Prepare the bed with a 7.5cm (3in) layer of compacted hardcore or scalping. The slabs are laid directly on top. For extra stability, put five spots of mortar on the sand.

2 Lay a single row of slabs in each direction, using taut string as a guide. Drop the slabs flat into place, trying not to drop one edge first. Tamp down each slab and check the level, in both directions, with a spirit level.

3 If you decide not to butt the slabs right up against each other, use spacers – small pieces of wood about 1cm (½in) thick – to make sure that they are evenly spaced. Remove the spacers as you work.

4 Shortly after you have finished laying the slabs, brush a dry mortar mix between the cracks, but make sure that the surface of the slabs is brushed clean.

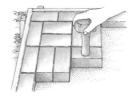

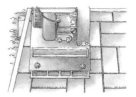

1 To prevent any outward movement of the surface, use edging restraints, which can be concreted in place, or sturdy, pressure-treated timber, at least 10cm (4in) deep and 4cm (1½in) thick, held in place by pegs, 5 x 5cm (2 x 2in).

2 On firm soil, a layer of sand 5cm (2in) deep will be a sufficient base. On softer soil, you will need 7.5cm (3in) of compacted scalpings beneath the sand. Bricks can also be laid on a layer of mortar about 2.5cm (1in) deep.

3 Paviors are bedded in sand. You will need to hire a plate compactor, which is used to settle the paviors into the sand and make sure they are level. Lay the paviors in position and use a club hammer to tamp them into place.

4 Brush dry sand over the surface, then use the plate compactor to bed them down.

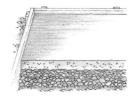

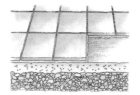

1 Prepare a well-consolidated base of scalpings 7.5cm (3in) deep, topped with 7.5cm (3in) of smooth surfaced concrete, which should be allowed to set.

2 Bed the tiles into a thin skim of mortar over the concrete base. Alternatively, use a proprietary outdoor tile adhesive, which should be applied to the base of each tile.

3 Quarry tiles can be finished by pointing with a suitably coloured mortar, while a special grouting material, suitable for outdoor use, should be used with glazed ceramic tiles.

Creeping or low-growing rock garden plants are ideal for planting in gaps between paving slabs.

- *Aethionema* 'Warley Rose'
- *Armeria maritima*
- *Aubrieta*
- *Campanula portenschlagiana*
- *Thymus* x *citriodorus*

It is probably a wise precaution to wear heavy-duty gloves to protect your hands when moving slabs. These will also protect your skin from the drying and roughening effects of mortar and cement.

SMALL UNIT PAVING

Small unit paving such as tiles, bricks and paviors are easier on the back than large paving slabs. On the other hand they are more time-consuming to lay, and more care needs to be taken to get a smooth, level surface. It is worth hiring a plate compactor to bed the units into the sand, as this makes a great difference to the appearance of the surface.

- Raised timber decking needs to be constructed on a framework of joists supported on concrete or brick foundations – a job for professionals. The lengths of timber should be laid with a 1cm (½in) gap between them to allow for drainage. Use brass screws or galvanized nails.
- Decking tiles are a more straightforward proposition. They can be laid on a firmly compacted base of 5cm (2in) sand in the same way as paviors, although they do not have to be bedded with a plate compactor. Use a spirit level on every tile to keep the surface level, and fix the tiles with angled nails.

GROWING PLANTS IN CONTAINERS

*T*here is one feature that all plant containers have in common: they hold a limited volume of compost. This may have a direct effect on the plant by restricting its root growth and consequently its overall size. Compost in containers is prone to drying out easily, and also to becoming waterlogged if the container is not raised up on 'feet'.

Water containers regularly to keep the compost moist at all times; in warm weather you must be prepared to do this once or even twice a day. Hanging baskets, which are exposed to the drying effects of the wind and sun on all sides, are especially vulnerable, and will need the most frequent watering to stop them becoming bone dry. Installing a pulley system to lower the basket, or using a hose with an extended lance, will help to make the chore of watering easier.

If soil-less composts have been used and no slow-release fertilizer has been incorporated, begin adding liquid fertilizer to the water shortly after planting the container. For flowering plants, use a high-potash fertilizer, such as tomato or rose food; for foliage plants, a general or high-nitrogen fertilizer should be used.

Provide plant supports as necessary, inserting them carefully before plants begin to flop. Position stakes unobtrusively and tie stems to them with soft twine. For spreading or climbing plants a trellis panel can be inserted into the compost in the container, or fixed in the ground or attached to a wall behind it.

ABOVE *If you do not have much time to spend on garden maintenance, restrict the number of containers to reduce the chore of watering, and pick easy-care plants.*

PROJECT	A SPRING WINDOWBOX

1 Lay a base of crocks, then half-fill the box with compost. Put evergreen trailers (such as ivy) at the edges, and insert winter-flowering heathers or a miniature conifer to fill the rest of the space.

2 Add in a selection of bulbs, such as crocuses and miniature daffodils. Trickle compost around the plants and over the bulbs, making sure it filters down between them, then firm it down gently and level off.

3 Water the completed box. If it is to sit on a sloping window ledge, use wooden wedges under the front edge to make it level. To make the box more secure, attach it to brackets.

PROJECT **A TUB WITH SUMMER BEDDING**

1 Make sure that there are sufficient drainage holes in the base of the tub and cover them with a layer of drainage material, such as crocks or stones. This will allow excess water to percolate through to the base of the tub but stop the compost from being washed away.

2 Tip in an appropriate compost – either soil-based or soil-less. This is also a good time to add slow-release fertilizer and water-retaining granules if you wish, mixing them thoroughly with the compost. Fill the tub almost, but not right up to, the top and level the surface.

3 Set the bedding plants, still in their pots, on the surface of the compost until you are satisfied with the arrangement. Place the upright plants in the centre and trailers round the edge.

4 One by one, knock each plant out of its pot by tapping it gently.

5 Plant using a trowel, filling in with more compost as necessary. Firm all the plants lightly into place with your knuckles. There should be a gap of about 1cm (⅓in) between the surface of the compost and the top of the tub to allow for watering.

6 Water the completed tub from overhead, using a fine rose on the watering can. Leave it in a sheltered, lightly shaded place for a day or two before setting it in its permanent position.

PROJECT **A TRADITIONAL WIRE HANGING BASKET**

1 Line the basket with moss or a proprietary liner, placing a saucer or square of plastic at the base to retain water. Fill the basket about one-third full of compost.

2 Wrap the roots of trailing plants in cones of newspaper. Push through the liner. Remove the paper and cover the roots with compost. Continue until the basket is three-quarters full.

3 Arrange plants on the top, using an upright plant in the centre to give height. Water the basket thoroughly. Keep sheltered and lightly shaded for two days before hanging out.

STAR PLANTS

Bulbs bring some of the earliest flowers of the year, always welcome after the dull days of winter.

- *Anemone blanda*
- *Chionodoxa luciliae*
- *Crocus chrysanthus*
- *Eranthis hyemalis*
- *Erythronium dens-canis*
- *Fritillaria meleagris*
- *Galanthus nivalis*
- *Iris histrioides*
- *Narcissus* spp.
- *Tulipa* spp.

MAKING A RAISED BED

Containers are perhaps the most popular way to grow plants in patio and courtyard gardens, but the role that can be played by beds and borders should not be overlooked. They make it possible to grow larger plants, they require less watering and feeding and they allow attractive planting schemes and plant associations to be enjoyed. Well-planted beds are also helpful in softening the sometimes harsh and un-welcoming appearance of paved areas.

Raised beds allow plants to grow where it is impossible to break up the surface of the patio, they add a valuable three-dimensional visual element to the patio garden, and their height makes them easier to plant and maintain.

There are two types of raised bed: those built on soil and those built on the surface of a patio. The benefits of a raised bed with a soil base are that the bed behaves more like a bed in the open garden — it is less prone both to drying out and to waterlogging. The roots of plants can penetrate more deeply into the ground, allowing larger plants such as trees to develop more fully. However, raised beds on the patio suface provide an opportunity to grow a collection of specialist plants such as alpines or moisture-loving subjects. Lining the bed with punctured polythene and filling it with moisture-retentive compost provides a good home for plants that thrive in marshy conditions, such as hostas, astilbes and some irises and primulas. A gritty, free-draining compost topped with fine gravel is ideal for alpines such as gentians, campanulas, saxifrages, lewisias and many others. Rhododendrons, azaleas, pieris, camellias and other plants that cannot tolerate lime in the soil will grow well in a raised bed that has been filled with ericaceous (lime-free) compost.

Adequate drainage must be provided for raised beds — a layer of coarse rubble should be used in the base, and weep holes must be established to allow excess water to drain away. Like any container, the beds are prone to waterlogging and rapid drying out, and the roots of plants within them are restricted in their growth.

The beds should be constructed of a material that is appropriate to their surroundings. Brick, concrete, reconstituted stone and natural stone blocks are popular choices, and railway sleepers are ideal for low beds. Medium-sized sawn logs, set upright in the ground, create a rustic-style bed. The size can vary according to your requirements,

ABOVE *The walling material of a raised bed can be made into a feature, like the weathered horizontal boards used here.*

but the normal minimum height is about 45cm (18in). Walls higher than 60cm (2ft) will require concrete footings. Do not make the beds so large that you cannot easily reach across them to plant and weed.

TYPES OF SOIL

The ideal garden soil is a friable loam containing plenty of organic matter, but few gardens are blessed with the ideal. There are three basic types of soil: sand, clay and loam.

Sandy soils consist of large particles, so that the soil drains very freely and dries out quickly. Plant nutrients are usually washed away by the drainage water, so sandy soils tend to be low in fertility. On the plus side, they are light and easy to work and warm up quickly in spring.

Clay soil consists of very small, fine particles, which cling together and make a sticky, slow-draining mass. Heavy, clay soils are often rich and fertile, and they hold water well in dry weather. However, when they do dry out, they can bake hard and become almost impossible to break up with a spade.

Loam is a nicely balanced mixture of clay and sand, giving a crumbly textured soil that is reasonably light to work while not drying out too quickly. A good loam soil also contains rotted organic matter – decomposed plant matter or animal manure – which supplies humus. This acts like a sponge to regulate the water and nutrient supply in the soil, as well as adding fertility.

All soils can be greatly improved by the regular addition of well-rotted organic matter. This can be provided by the garden compost heap or by purchasing 'soil improvers' from the garden centre. Using a balanced fertilizer for general growth and a high-potash one for flowering and fruiting plants is also recommended.

RAISED BED MADE FROM TIMBER

Before beginning construction, select an area of the garden that will provide a firm base for your raised bed, keeping in mind the types of plant you intend to grow in the construction (consider factors such as the amount of sunlight required). Purchase lengths of 10 x 12.5cm (4 x 5in) treated timber to make the frame for the raised bed.

PROJECT | **CONSTRUCTING A RAISED BED USING TIMBER**

1 Bond timber in staggered rows, like bricks. Drill holes through the wood and drive steel rods through the timber and about 20–30cm (8–12in) into the ground. Treat with a bitumastic paint on the inside to delay the process of rotting.

2 As an extra measure to combat decay, insert small sections of plumbing piping through the wood about 5cm (2in) from the base. This will aid drainage.

3 Fill the base of the bed with rubble for good drainage and top with geotextile membrane. If the bed is on a solid surface, this layer should occupy about one-third of its depth. If you wish to grow lime-hating plants, make sure the rubble is lime-free.

4 Choose the type of compost to suit the plants you intend to grow and fill the bed to within 10cm (4in) of the top. Set the plants in position on the surface of the compost first, so that they can be easily arranged to your satisfaction.

5 Use taller plants towards the centre or back of the bed, and set some trailers near the edges. Use a trowel to plant, and firm the plants in well using your knuckles.

6 When the planting is complete, water the bed thoroughly, preferably with a hose fitted with a fine spray.

HINTS AND TIPS

✿ Bagged compost is usually sold in litres, and the number of litres you will need can be calculated by multiplying together the depth, width and height of the bed in centimetres and dividing the result by 1,000. Topsoil is usually sold by the cubic metre or, occasionally, by the tonne. To estimate the number of cubic metres that will be needed, measure the depth, width and height of the bed in metres, multiply these dimensions together and divide the result by 9. One cubic metre of soil weighs approximately 1 tonne, although this varies according to the soil's moisture content.

CLIMBERS

*C*limbing plants help to make a patio garden truly three-dimensional. They make use of growing space that would otherwise be wasted – always an important consideration in a small garden – and help to provide living 'walls' to give the garden a secluded, protected and intimate feel. When they are trained across the top of a pergola, they can even provide a living 'roof' for the garden. Unsightly features can also be disguised by climbers.

The most obvious place to grow climbing plants is against a wall – a house wall, if a patio garden adjoins the house, or a garden wall. This is not only a good way to display the plants, but it helps to make the walls a real part of the garden, instead of just being a boundary.

If there are no walls, there are many other opportunities to place climbing plants. Fences, as long as they are in good repair, can support climbers just as easily as walls. Hedges, more surprisingly perhaps, often benefit from having climbing plants scrambling through them. This can give rise to some classic combinations, such as the glowing red flowers of nasturtium (*Tropaeolum speciosum*) spangled through a hedge of dark yew (*Taxus* spp.), but you must make sure that the climber you choose is not so vigorous that it will swamp its host.

Stone or brick pillars that form part of the structure of a house or an adjoining building make excellent supports for plants and could also be purpose-built as part of the patio garden. A wooden pergola is cheaper and easier to construct, and plants will not only clothe the uprights but also drape themselves over the horizontal beams, providing shade overhead and a degree of protection from light rain.

A plant-covered wood or metal arch will make the ideal entrance to, or exit from, a patio garden. Height can be added to raised beds or groups of containers simply by training plants over a wigwam of bamboo canes, tied together at their tips.

Climbing plants do not necessarily have to climb. Some types make very successful ground cover when allowed to sprawl over the surface of a bed. They may also be grown in a raised position and allowed to trail, which can be very attractive, forming billows of informal growth that provides a softening effect on the garden's features.

CLIMBERS IN CONTAINERS

Many climbers can be grown very successfully in containers. The growth of more vigorous subjects will be restricted so that they are easier to keep under control, and tender climbers, which cannot survive the winter outside, can be brought under cover in autumn, having enjoyed the summer out of doors. A classic-shaped container, such as an urn or wine jar, looks particularly attractive with a climbing plant cascading from its lip, giving the impression of flowing water. See pages 54–55 for advice on planting up a container.

PLANTING IN THE GROUND

As long as there is reasonable quality soil beneath the patio surface, a relatively small planting hole can be made for a climber. The roots will soon spread beneath the paving. Clematis, in particular, enjoys such conditions – it likes to have its top in the sun while its roots are cool and shady. More information on planting under the patio surface is given on the opposite page.

RIGHT *Honeysuckle,* Lonicera periclymenum, *is a traditional favourite, with flowers that have a strong, sweet scent.*

SUPPORTS AND TRAINING

A few plants are self-supporting, but the majority of climbing plants need a trellis or similar support. The size of the support required depends on the ultimate size of the plant. Check in a good reference book before planting.

Long vine eyes can be screwed into a wall, fence or blocks of wood attached to the wall. Wire is threaded through to provide horizontal supports. You should provide at least three horizontal wires, spaced about 45cm (18in) apart, along which the plant can be trained.

Trellis panels, made from wooden or plastic lathes, are available in a variety of shapes. Some are freestanding, although most are attached to a wall or fence. In order for the trellis to be taken down if necessary for maintenance purposes, it should be screwed to vertical wooden battens, which are themselves screwed to the wall. The battens should be at least 5cm (2in) deep to give good clearance behind the trellis. Plastic-covered wire trellis is available in rolls and is useful if you have to cover large areas. It can also be tacked round posts for plants to cling to.

Some trellis panels are specially made for use in containers, and these should be put in position in the tub before you begin to add the compost. Use a heavy, soil-based compost rather than a light, soil-less one.

PROJECT   **PLANTING CLIMBERS AGAINST WALLS**

STAR PLANTS

- Clematis spp. and cvs.
- Clianthus puniceus
- Cobaea scandens
- Eccremocarpus scaber
- Hedera helix
- Humulus lupulus 'Aureus'
- Jasminum officinale
- Lathyrus odoratus
- Lonicera periclymenum
- Parthenocissus henryana
- Passiflora caerulea
- Tropaeolum majus
- Vitis coignetiae
- Wisteria sinensis

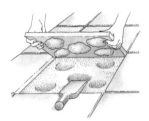

1 When you have decided where you want to place the climber, lift or break up the patio surface to give a planting area about 30cm (12in) square.

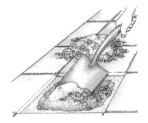

2 Make the planting hole about 45cm (18in) away from the base of the wall, which avoids the wall's foundations and allows the plant's roots to receive more rainwater than they would if they were directly in the lee of the wall.

3 Dig down to a spade's depth to make sure the soil is well broken and free draining, and, if the soil is poor, replace some of it with good quality topsoil. Add an application of a slow-release fertilizer, such as bonemeal.

4 Set the plant in the soil and, before firming in well, check that it is angled so that it leans towards the wall. You may need to insert a cane to support the plant until it reaches the wires or trellis you have already provided. Water thoroughly.

5 After planting, some of the paving material can be returned to cover the soil without damaging the plant's stem, or gravel or pebbles can be used instead to cover the soil surface, which will retain moisture in the soil and limit weed growth.

A PATIO WATER GARDEN

Any garden will be enhanced by the addition of a water feature. It does not have to be anything ornate: simple features are extremely effective. On a hot summer's day, the melodious sound of rippling water is instantly refreshing. In a small patio area, a formal sunken pool is an attractive and easy way of introducing the wonderful element of water into the garden. It can usually be built quite easily over a weekend.

A formal sunken pool is a relatively straightforward feature to incorporate into a patio garden. Choose an open, sunny position where there are not a lot of overhanging trees – their falling leaves will cause problems in autumn – and make the dimensions of the pool as large as practical. Although pre-formed rigid pools may at first appear to be the easiest option, a pool made with a flexible liner is in fact far quicker and simpler to install. Black liners, or those

made in dark colours, give a much more satisfactory result than the pale blue ones that are often on sale.

In order to keep the water clear, plants for the pool should include oxygenators, submerged aquatic plants that supply the water with oxygen, and aquatics with floating leaves, which shade the water and prevent excessive algal growth. Among useful oxygenators are the pondweed *Lagarosiphon major* and ferny *Myriophyllum spicatum*. Plants with floating leaves include the ever-popular waterlilies and white-flowered, fragrant water hawthorn (*Aponogeton distachyos*).

Fish add extra life and interest to the pond as well as having the practical purpose of controlling the mosquitoes and midges which otherwise breed there. Feed fish during the summer months to build them up to survive the winter; they will soon learn to come and take food from the hand, which increases their appeal.

When constructing a pond, clear the area where the pool is to be constructed, lifting paving slabs and so on as necessary. You will need to extend the clear area well beyond the ultimate extent of the pond. Check that the site is absolutely level, then dig out the hole.

WATCHPOINTS

❧ Butyl rubber is one of the best choices for this type of pond. Heavy-duty laminated PVC is a popular, slightly cheaper alternative. These liners usually have a guaranteed life of 15–25 years. Don't be tempted by much cheaper polythene – its very short life makes it a false economy.

LEFT *The distinctive white edging to this pond emphasizes its undulating shape, and is complemented by the low-growing plants that border it. A central fountain brings it to life.*

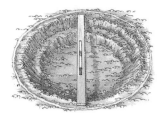

1 Dig out the soil to a depth of at least 45cm (18in). The sides should slope slightly, to around 20°. Allow for a shelf for marginal plants about 25cm (10in) wide and 22cm (9in) below the water surface (this need only run round part of the pool).

2 Remove debris, smooth and compact the surface, and use soft sand or layers of newspaper to line the excavation, thus making sure that protruding sharp stones or roots cannot puncture the liner. Check again that the top of the pond is absolutely level.

3 Calculate the size of liner needed by this formula: pond width + (depth x 2) x pond length + (depth x 2). Allow a 20cm (8in) overlap around the pond. Lay the liner evenly over the excavation and let it sag into the hole. Use bricks to hold it in place.

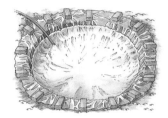

4 Begin filling the pool with a gently running hose. The weight of the water will gradually stretch the liner to fit the excavation perfectly. As the pond fills, the weights holding the liner in place can gradually be eased off.

5 Once the pond is full, trim the edges of the liner to leave around 15cm (6in) of overlap round the edge. Any folds in the overlap can be cut to lie flat, but be careful not to cut too close to the edge of the pool. Cover the overlap with an even layer of soil.

6 Finish the edge of the pool neatly with bricks or paving slabs. These should be laid so that they overlap the pool edge by about 5cm (2in), and must be bedded on cement to ensure they are firm and stable. Take care not to drop cement into the pool.

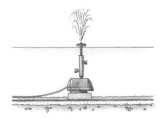

7 Moving water introduces vitality to a pond. A submersible pump is the simplest type for a small pond; it is simply submerged in the pool, standing on bricks or stones to raise it above the level of the mud at the bottom.

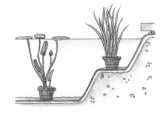

8 Aquatic plants should be planted in pond planting crates. Line the crates with hessian and set the plants firmly in good-quality heavy loam, topped off with gravel. Water well and lower the planted crates slowly to the base of the pond.

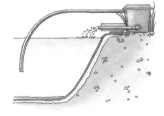

9 The water in a newly filled and planted pond will often become bright green and murky after a few days, as an explosion of algal growth takes place. This should clear after a few days: if algae persist, a small filter unit can be helpful.

THE MIDNIGHT GARDEN

*B*ringing *lighting outdoors adds an almost ethereal quality to a garden and means that you can continue to enjoy this outside room long after dusk. A lit garden will enhance the quality of your leisure time by freeing up those dark hours that previously confined you indoors. Instead of spending another evening slumped in front of the television, unwind by strolling round the garden with a glass of claret in hand.*

Look out for wall-mounted lamps as well as those on stakes, and decide if you want all-round illumination or a directional beam. Coloured and frosted lenses give quite different results from plain glass. Most path or marker lights look decorative because the unit itself is on view and forms part of the feature. With floodlights or spotlights, however, the aim is usually to draw attention from the source of the light, which is often concealed, to the feature being illuminated.

Of the three main ways of using spotlights, perhaps the most popular is to position them at ground level and point the adjustable head towards a feature. Downlighting usually gives a softer, less dramatic effect. With this style of lighting, the spotlight is mounted on a wall or tall stake so that the light shines down onto a feature. Backlighting is more difficult to achieve successfully than either uplighting or down-lighting. The spotlight is

RIGHT *Temporary lighting effects can be achieved with candles, lanterns and garden flares, which add a romantic touch.*

PROJECT **BURYING AN ARMOURED CABLE FOR A GARDEN POWER SUPPLY**

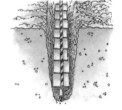

1 When installing lighting for pools, you need to dig a trench for the armoured cable. This should to be a minimum of 1m (3ft) deep and 20–25cm (8–10in) wide.

2 Place the cable inside a length of plastic conduit and then cover the cable with roof tiles for extra protection.

3 Ensure that the tiles are securely in place and tape them down with a piece of highly coloured warning tape that tells you there is an electrical supply near by.

4 Fill the trench with soil. You will need to get an electrician to connect the cable to a circuit breaker and transformer, so a low-voltage lighting system can be used.

fixed behind the feature to throw it into silhouette, which is particularly effective with strongly architectural shapes. It is important to avoid glare from some angles of view.

With all three types of lighting, simply changing the angle of the spotlight and the distance between the lamp and the feature can significantly alter the effects achieved. Go out in the evening and experiment with different arrangements before you actually fix the lamps in place, to make sure that you end up with exactly the effect you want. Rather than risk potential danger, seek professional help if you have no experience with electrical installations. If you are using lighting in water, be sure to purchase a kit specifically designed for use in water.

WATCHPOINTS

⬧ Select a kit which contains an appropriate number of lamps and length of cable. The maximum number of lamps you will be able to run depends on the total output of the bulbs used and the maximum loading on the transformer. For example, if the transformer is rated at 42 watts, you can use it to run six lights fitted with 7-watt bulbs, but you could increase this to 10 lights if they were fitted with 4-watt bulbs.
⬧ Bear in mind when installing a low-watt lighting system that the voltage will drop slightly as it travels along the cable, so that lamps at the far end of a long cable run will be less bright than those nearest the transformer.

PROJECT INSTALLING A LOW-VOLTAGE (12v) LIGHTING SYSTEM

1 Decide where lights are required and make a small plan. Estimate the length of cable required by running a piece of string from the power socket along the proposed route, remembering to allow for concealing the cable.

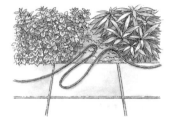

2 Allow enough cable for the lamps also. Lay out the cable over the route. Lamps can be attached at any point: the usual method is to loop the cable, pushing the loop through the base of the light unit until it makes contact with the terminal pins.

3 A screw-cap or cam is then used to force the pins into the cable to make the electrical contact. The rest of the lighting head is then assembled and fitted, and the light positioned by pushing the ground stake firmly into the soil.

4 If you change your mind about the position of the lights it is easy to move them; just cover the holes made by the pins in the cable with insulating tape to keep out moisture and dirt.

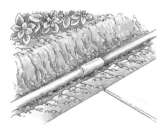

5 Position the transformer in a suitable spot, according to the instructions. Once you have tested the system, bury the cable shallowly where it runs over the soil, where it will not be damaged later by digging.

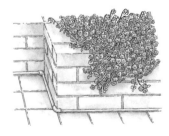

6 Extra length of cable may be necessary to allow you to run it round the edges of paved areas and raised beds, though for a permanent system you may wish to run the cable underneath paving slabs.

THE PLANT DIRECTORY

Perhaps the most important issue to bear in mind in selecting plants for patio and courtyard gardens is scale. Some thought will have to be given to the potential size of the plants you choose if your space is not to be overwhelmed by an over-large shrub or tree. The plants in the directory are all suitable for use in a limited space, or for growing in pots and other containers.

LEFT *A haze of blue, mauve and pink delicately clothes a patio garden where the designer has made the most of the available space by setting in raised beds and adding a pergola for vertical planting.*

HOW TO USE THIS DIRECTORY

*T*he Plant Directory lists all the plants that are featured in this book, together with a selection of other plants that are suitable for use in a patio garden. It is not intended to be exhaustive, and experienced gardeners will have their own favourites. However, this listing has been made with the specific requirements of a patio garden in mind, and will guide the beginner to a range of attractive and readily available plants, shrubs and trees with which to create a beautiful garden. Complete information on planting and maintaining the plants is given for each entry.

The Plant Directory is divided into different categories that group like plants together. The categories are annuals and biennials, including tender perennials used as annuals *(page 68)*, bulbs, corms and tubers *(page 76)*, herbaceous perennials *(page 80)*, grasses, bamboos and ferns *(page 88)*, conifers *(page 89)*, climbers *(page 90)*, tender shrubs and perennials *(page 92)*, and trees and shrubs *(page 94)*.

The plants have been chosen for their moderate habit or speed of growth which means that they are suitable for use in small spaces. Several of the plants chosen are able to be pruned to adapt them to a limited area. The symbols panel accompanying each entry gives essential information on the plant's preferred growing conditions, its potential size and its season of interest.

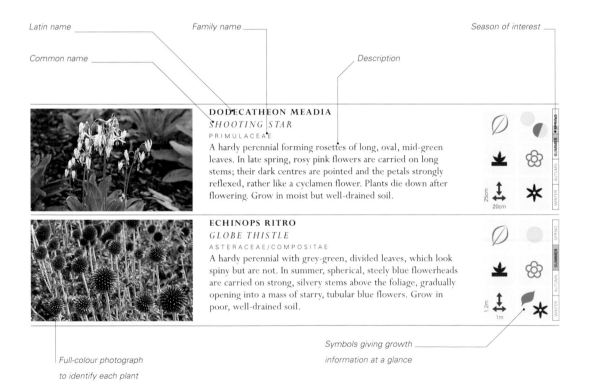

Latin name

Common name

Family name

Description

Season of interest

DODECATHEON MEADIA
SHOOTING STAR
PRIMULACEAE
A hardy perennial forming rosettes of long, oval, mid-green leaves. In late spring, rosy pink flowers are carried on long stems; their dark centres are pointed and the petals strongly reflexed, rather like a cyclamen flower. Plants die down after flowering. Grow in moist but well-drained soil.

ECHINOPS RITRO
GLOBE THISTLE
ASTERACEAE/COMPOSITAE
A hardy perennial with grey-green, divided leaves, which look spiny but are not. In summer, spherical, steely blue flowerheads are carried on strong, silvery stems above the foliage, gradually opening into a mass of starry, tubular blue flowers. Grow in poor, well-drained soil.

Full-colour photograph
to identify each plant

Symbols giving growth
information at a glance

KEY TO THE SYMBOLS

 EASY TO GROW

These are tolerant plants that require no special care or conditions in order to flourish.

 MODERATE TO GROW

These are plants that require some special care, such as protection from frost.

 DIFFICULT TO GROW

These are plants that require a great deal of specialized care, and offer a challenge for the more experienced gardener.

 EVERGREEN

 SEMI-EVERGREEN

 DECIDUOUS

Deciduous plants lose all their leaves in autumn (sometimes in summer), while evergreen plants keep their foliage all year. Plants described as semi-evergreen may keep some or all of their foliage through the winter in sheltered gardens or if the weather is mild. No leaf symbol is given for annuals, nor for biennials, although some biennials do keep their leaves over the first winter.

 FEATURE LEAVES

 FEATURE SCENT

 FEATURE FLOWER

 FEATURE FRUIT

These symbols indicate the main feature of interest for each plant in the directory, although this is not necessarily the plant's only attractive asset. Some plants are given more than one symbol. This information will help you to choose plants that have complementary features, or plants that will perform a specific function in your garden.

 RAPID GROWTH

 MODERATE GROWTH

 SLOW GROWTH

Speed of growth, like ease of growth, is a highly subjective category, and will vary according to local conditions. Rapid growth indicates plants that reach their full extent in a single season (annuals for instance), or plants that make substantial progress towards filling the space allowed for them in a single season. Slow growth indicates plants, such as trees and some shrubs, that take several seasons to reach their ultimate size. Moderate growth relates therefore to rates of progress between these two extremes.

SEASON OF INTEREST

The period of the year when a plant is likely to be most attractive is also indicated in a vertical bar to the right of each entry. Those plants that have something to offer all year round are marked accordingly. This will help you in creating a planting plan for each season.

 HEIGHT AND SPREAD

The size of plants will vary according to the growing conditions in your garden, so these measurements are a rough guide only. The measurements refer to the size of plants and trees when mature, although there are specific circumstances where the ultimate size is never reached.

 FULL SUN

 PARTIAL SUN

 SHADE

An indication of light preference is given to show each plant's optimum growing situation. Here again, this is only a rough guide, as some plants that prefer sun may also be reasonably tolerant of shade.

ANNUALS AND BIENNIALS

AGERATUM HOUSTONIANUM 'BLUE DANUBE'
FLOSSFLOWER
ASTERACEAE

A low-growing annual that forms a compact hummock of mid-green leaves, topped with fluffy, lilac-blue flowerheads. A good edging plant for borders and containers. Pink and white forms are also available, but blue is the most popular colour. Grow in a fertile, moist but well-drained soil.

15cm / 15cm

AMARANTHUS CAUDATUS
LOVE-LIES-BLEEDING
AMARANTHACEAE

A half-hardy annual with light green, ovate leaves, *Amaranthus* is grown for its showy, drooping, deep red tassels of flowers, which can reach 45cm (18in) in length. Plants are particularly good for the edges of raised beds or containers, where the flowers can trail freely. Grow in humus-rich, moist, fertile soil.

1m / 45cm

ANAGALLIS 'SKYLOVER'
PIMPERNEL
PRIMULACEAE

Although *Anagallis* is perennial, it is best treated as an annual. The leaves are linear, carried in whorls along spreading, lax, slender stems. The gentian-blue flowers have rose-pink and gold centres, and are freely produced. Likes fertile, moist but well-drained soil. Good for the front of a border or for a rock garden.

23cm / 45cm

ANGELONIA GARDNERI
SCROPHULARIACEAE

Part of a genus of around 30 species of sub-shrubs and evergreen plants. This tender perennial has lance-shaped, slightly hairy leaves and in summer produces purple flowers with white disc florets. These can reach up to 15cm (6in) high. Originally from Brazil, this species likes a soil that is moist, fertile and well drained. Good for a border.

1m / 30cm

ANTIRRHINUM MAJUS
SNAPDRAGON
SCROPHULARIACEAE

Short-lived perennials that are usually grown as annuals. They have tubular and pouched flowers with two prominent lips, and cultivars are available in almost every colour, plus varieties with contrasting coloured veining. Dwarf varieties are ideal for containers. Grow in well-drained, fertile soil.

20cm / 30cm

ARCTOTIS X HYBRIDA
AFRICAN DAISY
ASTERACEAE

Half-hardy perennials usually grown as annuals, African daisies produce large, colourful, daisy-like flowers at the top of tall stems. Lobed leaves are silver-grey. Flower colours include red, rose-pink, orange and white. Flowers will open fully only in direct sun. Grow in sharply drained soil.

45cm / 45cm

≣ leaf type   ● light preference   ♀ speed of growth   ✿ ease of growth

BELLIS PERENNIS
DOUBLE DAISY
ASTERACEAE

A perennial usually grown as a biennial. Can have a mass of small, button flowers ('Pomponette') or larger blooms (such as 'Goliath' or Habanera Series). Flowers generally have the central yellow disc typical of daisies replaced by tightly grouped petals in red, pink or white. Likes a fertile, moist but well-drained soil.

20cm / 20cm

BIDENS FERULIFOLIA
TICKSEED
ASTERACEAE

A half-hardy annual producing a mass of delicate, ferny foliage on sprawling stems, studded with a profusion of golden, star shaped flowers throughout the summer. Easy to grow in most conditions – flowers well even in poor weather. Grow in a soil that is quite fertile and moist but well drained.

45cm / 45cm

BRACHYSCOME MULTIFIDA
ROCK DAISY
ASTERACEAE

Originally from parts of southeast Australia, this annual has finely divided leaves which are joined by blue, pink, purple or white flowers from midsummer to mid-autumn. A good plant to grow in containers, in a border or in a rock garden, it likes fertile, well-drained but moist soil.

45cm / 45cm

CHRYSANTHEMUM – FLORIST'S HYBRIDS
ASTERACEAE

Part of a genus of around 20 upright annuals and tender perennials. These cultivars come in many colours and are grown for cutting and exhibition as well as for the garden. Flowering periods vary from late summer and early autumn to mid-autumn and midwinter. Likes a neutral to slightly acid soil that is fertile, moist but well drained.

1.2m / 60cm

CLARKIA AMOENA
GODETIA
ONAGRACEAE

A hardy annual that makes bushy growth, with slender, lanceolate leaves and a profusion of open, cup-shaped, silky-textured flowers. Flowers are single, double or semi-double (azalea flowered), in a range of red, pink and lavender shades. Grow in moist but well-drained, fertile, slightly acid soil.

30–60cm / 30cm

COBAEA SCANDENS
CUP-AND-SAUCER PLANT
COBAEACEAE

A tender perennial climber usually grown as a half hardy annual. Its leaves are rich green and have tiny hooks. From summer to autumn, it produces bell-shaped flowers, which begin life green and turn purple. Grow in a moist but well-drained, fertile soil.

4m / 2m

---

 height and spread   feature of interest   ▨ season of interest   *ANNUALS AND BIENNIALS* **A – C**

ANNUALS AND BIENNIALS

CONVOLVULUS SABATIUS
BINDWEED
CONVOLVULACEAE

A creeping or trailing, rather tender perennial, frequently grown as an annual. The small, oval leaves are a silvery green. Satin-textured, trumpet-shaped, clear blue flowers are freely carried along the stems throughout summer. Grow in gritty, moderately fertile, well-drained soil.

15cm / 60cm

COSMOS ASTROSANGUINEUS
CHOCOLATE COSMOS
ASTERACEAE

A half-hardy perennial that produces a mound of attractive, finely cut, deep green foliage. The elegant, saucer-shaped flowers, carried on tall stems above the leaves, are a striking deep maroon shade and have an unusual scent of bitter chocolate. Grow in fertile, moist but well-drained soil.

60cm / 45cm

DIASCIA 'CORAL BELLE' (SYN. 'HECBEL')
DIASCIA
SCROPHULARIACEAE

A perennial often grown as an annual, diascia makes spreading, lax growth, with mid- to deep green, ovate leaves and dense clusters of lipped flowers with golden stamens. *D.* 'Coral Belle' has flowers of a clear, deep salmon shade on a compact plant. Grow in moist, well-drained, fertile soil.

20cm / 30cm

DIGITALIS PURPUREA – FOXY HYBRIDS GROUP
FOXGLOVE
SCROPHULARIACEAE

One of a genus of biennials and perennials found around Europe, Northern Africa and Asia, this plant has rosette-forming, hairy leaves but is grown for its flowers. These arrive in early summer, and come in shades of yellow, white, purple or pink. This variety can be grown as an annual. Grow in any soil.

90cm / 30cm

DOROTHEANTHUS BELLIDIFORMIS
LIVINGSTONE DAISY
AIZOACEAE

An annual with cylindrical, spoon-shaped, light green leaves. In summer, it bears a profusion of white, crimson, red, orange and yellow flowers. A good plant to grow in a border, in cracks in the paving or in a rock garden. Prefers a soil that is well drained and sandy, and not fertile.

15cm / 30cm

FELICIA AMELLOIDES
BLUE DAISY
ASTERACEAE

Originally from South Africa, this sub-shrub is usually grown as an annual. It has deep green, ovate to obovate leaves, and from summer to autumn it will bear light to darker blue flowerheads. Good for a rock garden, a raised bed or the base of a wall, this plant likes a poor, well-drained soil.

45cm / 45cm

🌿 leaf type   ● light preference   🌱 speed of growth   ⚙ ease of growth

GAZANIA 'AZTEC'
TREASURE FLOWER
ASTERACEAE

These perennials, which are grown as annuals, have lance-shaped, silver foliage and large, showy, daisy flowers with cream and purple-striped petals. Many other varieties exist, with flowers of yellow, orange, pink and white, the petals generally showing a darker zone around the central eye. Grow in light, sandy soil.

30cm / 30cm

HELICHRYSUM PETIOLARE
ASTERACEAE

This trailing evergreen has ovate to heart-shaped leaves, which are woolly on top. It produces white flowerheads in terminal corymbs in late summer and autumn. There are several forms with coloured or variegated leaves. The plant will do best in a soil that is well drained and moderately fertile

23cm / 1.2m

HELIOTROPIUM ARBORESCENS
CHERRY PIE, HELIOTROPE
BORAGINACEAE

Often grown as an annual, this perennial shrub with oval to lance-shaped, wrinkled green leaves that are often edged with purple. It is grown for its flowers, borne in summer, which are violet blue. Good for a container or a window box, this plant appreciates moist but well-drained, fertile soil.

45cm / 60cm

IMPATIENS CULTIVARS
BUSY LIZZY
BALSAMINACEAE

Tender perennials grown as annuals for colourful summer bedding. The succulent stems bear ovate, mid-green, toothed leaves and flat-faced, spurred flowers in summer. Colours include red, salmon, pink, white and orange; there are also double-flowered varieties. Grow in humus-rich, moist soil.

15–30cm / 15–30cm

IPOMOEA TRICOLOR 'HEAVENLY BLUE'
MORNING GLORY
CONVOLVULACEAE

Indigenous to tropical regions of Central and South America, this variety is usually grown as a fast-growing annual. Its heart-shaped leaves are joined by funnel-shaped, blue flowers in summer. A twining plant good for covering a pergola or an arch, and for providing ground cover. Grow in well-drained, fertile soil.

3m / 1m

LATHYRUS ODORATUS 'BIJOU'
SWEET PEA
PAPILIONACEAE

An annual bedding plant with mid-green leaflets and large, fragrant, pea-type flowers in summer. The colour range includes red, pink and lilac. *L. o.* 'Bijou' is a dwarf, bushy, non-climbing form: other varieties climb suitable supports by means of tendrils. Grow in humus-rich, fertile, well-drained soil.

45cm / 45cm

---

 height and spread ✳ feature of interest ▮▮▮ season of interest *ANNUALS AND BIENNIALS* **C – L**

ANNUALS AND BIENNIALS

LAURENTIA AXILLARIS
CAMPANULACEAE

A half-hardy annual, also known as *Solenopsis axillaris* and sometimes sold as *Isotoma axillaris*. An increasingly popular patio plant. Narrow, deep green leaves form a neat, domed mound. A profusion of slender-petalled, star-shaped flowers are carried on long, delicate stems, in shades of blue, pink or white; they are lightly scented. Grow in well-drained, moderately fertile soil.

30cm / 45cm

LAVATERA TRIMESTRIS
MALLOW
MALVACEAE

An annual that forms a bushy plant with light green, lobed leaves and numerous, trumpet-shaped, silky-petalled flowers from midsummer into autumn. Blooms may be white ('Dwarf White Cherub', 'Mont Blanc') or rosy pink ('Pink Beauty', 'Silver Cup'). Likes light, moderately fertile, well-drained soil.

35-60cm / 35-45cm

LOBELIA ERINUS
LOBELIA
CAMPANULACEAE

A half-hardy perennial usually grown as a half-hardy annual, forming a small, compact bush. It has bronzy-green, lance-shaped leaves and blue or purple flowers. There are trailing varieties of lobelia such as 'Blue Cascade', which are particularly suitable for hanging baskets. Likes fertile, moist soil.

15cm / 15cm

LOTUS BERTHELOTII
PARROT'S BEAK
PAPILIONACEAE

A tender perennial that is becoming increasingly popular as a hanging basket plant. It has whorls of silvery, needle-like leaves; and in shelter during a warm summer it bears unusual, claw-like orange-red flowers. Overwinter in a frost-free place, or treat as an annual. Grow in moderately fertile, well-drained soil.

23cm / 45cm

MATTHIOLA BICORNIS
NIGHT-SCENTED STOCK
BRASSICACEAE

An erect, spreading annual indigenous to Greece and south west Asia. It has narrow grey-green leaves and in summer it produces open racemes of pink, mauve or purple flowers that are fragrant at night. It prefers a neutral to alkaline, fertile, moist but well-drained soil.

35cm / 20cm

MYOSOTIS 'BLUE BALL'
FORGET-ME-NOT
BORAGINACEAE

A perennial usually grown as a biennial for spring bedding. The lance-shaped, soft green leaves are topped by spikes of small, blue, white-eyed flowers in spring. They mix well with spring bulbs such as tulips. Plants are prone to mildew in overcrowded conditions. Grow in poor, moist but well-drained soil.

15cm / 15cm

 leaf type    light preference   speed of growth   ease of growth

NEMESIA DENTICULATA
NEMISIA
SCROPHULARIACEAE

A perennial grown as an annual, *Nemesia* has toothed, lanceolate, mid-green leaves and clusters of pale lilac, lipped flowers with yellow markings on the lower petals. Its spreading habit makes it ideal for containers. *N. denticulata* is sometimes sold as *N. d.* 'Confetti'. Grow in moist, well-drained, slightly acid soil.

30cm
45cm

NICOTIANA DOMINO SERIES
FLOWERING TOBACCO
SOLANACEAE

A perennial plant that is treated as a half-hardy annual. The Domino Series is one of several compact, dwarf forms that keep their star-shaped, tubular flowers in mixed colours open all day instead of just in the evening. They are lightly fragrant, although some species, such as *N. affinis*, have a stronger, sweeter scent.

30cm
30cm

OSTEOSPERMUM 'BUTTERMILK'
ASTERACEAE

From a genus of plants indigenous to southern Africa and the Arabian peninsula, this type is an upright shrub with inversely lance-shaped, green leaves. From late spring to autumn, this plant produces daisy-like flowerheads with yellow florets. Good for a border or for a wall. This plant prefers a light soil that is moderately fertile and well drained.

60cm
30cm

PAPAVER NUDICAULE
ICELANDIC POPPY
PAPAVERACEAE

This hardy perennial is often short-lived and is sometimes treated as an annual or biennial. It forms a rosette of deeply lobed, light green leaves, and in summer bears single flowers of a typical, open poppy shape, in shades of white, yellow, orange and red. Likes a deep, fertile and well-drained soil.

45cm
30cm

PELARGONIUM CULTIVARS
GERANIUM
GERANIACEAE

Tender perennials, often grown as annuals, pelargoniums are the summer mainstay of many containers. Zonal varieties have rounded, aromatic leaves and brightly coloured flowers in round heads: trailing ivy-leaved types have ivy-shaped leaves and less dense flowerheads. Grow in neutral to alkaline, fertile soil.

15-60cm
15-60cm

PETUNIA HYBRIDA 'SURFINIA'
SOLANACEAE

These petunias grow more rapidly than other types and have branching habits. Flowers arrive in shades of white, pink, magenta, red, blue and violet. The plants are free-flowering and produce their blooms from late spring to late autumn. Because of its trailing habit, it is ideal for a hanging basket. Site in soil that is light and well drained.

30cm
1m

---

 height and spread   ✹ feature of interest   season of interest   *ANNUALS AND BIENNIALS* **L – P**

ANNUALS AND BIENNIALS

PORTULACA GRANDIFLORA
SUN PLANT
PORTULACACEAE

A half-hardy annual with lax and sprawling, succulent stems and bright green, pointed leaves. In summer, a mass of saucer-shaped flowers in red, pink, yellow, orange and white open in full sun. Flowers may be single or double, and have showy golden stamens. Likes poor, well-drained soil.

20cm
15cm

RUDBECKIA HYBRIDS
CONEFLOWER
ASTERACEAE

A short-lived perennial usually grown as an annual. The leaves are deep green, and the daisy-like flowers have rich golden petals and prominent, chocolate-brown central cones. This compact, dwarf variety is ideal for windowboxes and containers. Grow in heavy but well-drained, moderately fertile soil.

25cm
25cm

SALVIA SPLENDENS 'BLAZE OF FIRE'
SCARLET SAGE
LAMIACEAE

A half-hardy perennial often grown as an annual for colourful summer bedding. The ovate leaves are bright green with toothed margins, on compact, bushy plants. In summer, stiffly upright spikes of brilliant scarlet, tubular flowers and bracts are carried. Grow in light, humus-rich, well-drained soil.

25cm
20cm

SANVITALIA 'LITTLE SUN'
CREEPING ZINNIA
ASTERACEAE

A hardy annual with a bushy, lax habit, ideal for containers and hanging baskets. The foliage is a deep, bronzy-green, and the profuse daisy-like flowers are bright golden yellow. There is also an orange-flowered variety with green-centred blooms and mid-green leaves. Grow in fertile, humus-rich, well-drained soil.

20cm
45cm

SCAVEOLA AEMULA 'SAPHIRA'
BLUE FAN FLOWER
GOODENIACEAE

A tender perennial plant usually grown as an annual in containers and hanging baskets. Thick, sprawling stems bear lance-shaped leaves and large numbers of purple-blue, one-sided flowers with a pale eye. Likes moderately fertile, moist but well-drained, humus-rich soil.

25cm
1m

SENECIO CINERARIA 'SILVER DUST'
ASTERACEAE

From a genus of over 1,000 species, an evergreen shrub grown as an annual. Its attraction is its silvery ovate to lance-shaped leaves but the plant also bears yellow flowerheads in midsummer after the second year. Good for a container or a small rock garden, it likes a soil that is moderately fertile, gritty and well drained.

30cm
30cm

leaf type   light preference   ⚘ speed of growth   ✿ ease of growth

TAGETES 'TANGERINE GEM"
FRENCH MARIGOLD
ASTERACEAE

A half-hardy annual with deeply divided, mid-green leaves which are aromatic when touched. Plants make a rounded, bushy mound with flowers which are bright orange shading to yellow at the tips of the petals. Grows in almost any soil.

20cm
30cm

THUNBERGIA ALATA
BLACK-EYED SUSAN
ACANTHACEAE

An evergreen, twining climber, great for a border or for training against a wall or over an arch. It has triangular mid-green leaves and from summer to autumn it produces axillary flowers, orange or yellow and sometimes creamy white. These have dark brown centres. Likes moist, fertile, well-drained soil.

1.8m
60cm

TOLMIEA MENZIESII 'TAFF'S GOLD'
PICKABACK PLANT
SAXIFRAGACEAE

A hardy perennial, also available as *T. m.* 'Variegata', useful for hanging baskets. The mid-green leaves are heavily splashed and sprinkled with gold and soon form a dense mat. Young plants are formed at the bases of older leaves, weighing the leaves down to give a trailing effect. Grow in moist, humus-rich soil.

15cm
45cm

TORENIA FOURNIERI
WISHBONE FLOWER
SCROPHULARIACEAE

A half-hardy annual with green, toothed leaves on branching, rather lax, semi-trailing stems. Velvet-textured flowers are tubular and lipped; they may be white, pale blue or violet, often with darker markings on the lower lip. There is a yellow variety with brown markings. Likes fertile, moist but well-drained soil.

30cm
30cm

TROPAEOLUM MAJUS 'RED WONDER'
NASTURTIUM
TROPAEOLACEAE

A hardy annual with rounded, grey-green leaves and brilliant scarlet, double, trumpet-shaped flowers in summer. This bushy variety is ideal as an edging plant and for containers. There are also trailing varieties which are great for hanging baskets. Grow in a moderately fertile, moist but well-drained soil.

30cm
45cm

VERBENA 'SILVER ANNE'
VERBENA
VERBENACEAE

A half-hardy perennial that is generally grown as an annual. The leaves are oval and mid-green with serrated edges and are carried on trailing stems. Clusters of tubular, lobed flowers appear in summer and continue until autumn; they are soft pink and have a strong honey fragrance. Grow in a moderately fertile soil.

20cm
30cm

---

 height and spread   ✳ feature of interest   ▮▮▮ season of interest   *ANNUALS AND BIENNIALS* **P – V**

BULBS, CORMS AND TUBERS

ALLIUM MOLY
GOLDEN GARLIC
ALLIACEAE

Indigenous to regions of southern Europe, a bulbous perennial with grey-green leaves and, in summer, dense umbels of star-shaped, bright yellow flowers. Grow in a border or in a rock garden or raised bed. Choose a soil that is fertile and well drained and site in full sun.

ANEMONE BLANDA
WINDFLOWER
RANUNCULACEAE

A pretty, spreading tuberous perennial. This plant has dark green basal and stem leaves, and, in spring, deep blue flowers are borne with yellow centres. Good for a rock garden or a raised bed. Grow in a soil that is humus-rich, light and sandy and moist but well drained.

ARUM ITALICUM 'MARMORATUM'
LORDS AND LADIES
ARACEAE

A tuberous perennial with green, white-veined leaves that stay from winter to late spring. Its pale green flowers arrive in early summer, and are followed by bright orangey-red berries, which survive until the new leaves develop. Grow in well-drained, humus-rich soil in a sheltered site.

BEGONIA X TUBERHYBRIDA
BEGONIACEAE

Mostly bushy and upright tuberous perennials. They are prized for their leaves and flowers. Most produce flowers in the summer in small clusters. Good for pots, beds and borders they vary tremendously in habit from pendular to erect. Choose a soil for these plants that is slightly acid, fertile, humus-rich and moist but well drained.

CANNA HYBRIDS
INDIAN SHOT PLANT
CANNACEAE

These showy, tender perennials grow from rhizomatous roots. Very large, broad leaves clasp the stem and look similar to banana leaves; the foliage may be strikingly coloured or striped in some cultivars. The tall flower spike carries exotic-looking blooms in shades of red, orange and yellow.

CHIONODOXA LUCILIAE
GLORY OF THE SNOW
HYACINTHACEAE

A bulbous perennial with recurved leaves. In spring, it produces star-shaped, blue flowers with wide sepals. It is good for a rock garden, a raised bed, a sink garden or for planting under trees. This plant likes a well-drained soil in a position where it receives good sunlight.

🌿 leaf type   ⬤ light preference   🌱 speed of growth   ✿ ease of growth

COLCHICUM AUTUMNALE 'ALBUM'
MEADOW SAFFRON
COLCHICACEAE

A vigorous, cormous perennial with linear leaves and, in autumn, tubular white flowers. The species has lilac-coloured flowers. Good for a rock garden, a scree bed, a raised bed or a sink garden. This plant likes soil that is deep, fertile and well drained, and that will not dry out during summer.

15cm / 15cm

CRINUM X POWELLII
AMARYLLIDACEAE

Part of a genus of 130 species originally found near water in tropical regions of South Africa. It is a deciduous perennial with arching, mid-green leaves, and from summer to autumn it produces umbels of pale pink flowers. A good plant for a scree garden or for a sheltered border. Grow in deep, humus-rich, moist but well-drained, fertile soil.

60cm / 60cm

CROCOSMIA X CROCOSMIIFLORA
IRIDACEAE

Originally from South Africa, this tough, cormous perennial has long, pale green leaves and, in summer, spikes of orange to yellow flowers are produced. Good for the edge of a shrub border or for a herbaceous border. An excellent cut flower. Grow in soil that is moderately fertile, humus-rich, moist but well drained, and plant deep.

1m / 45cm

CROCUS CHRYSANTHUS
IRIDACEAE

A popular corm which produces grassy foliage and goblet-shaped, golden-yellow flowers in late winter and early spring. Hybrid cultivars are the most popular; their colours range from yellow to pale blue, lilac, purple and white. Yellow and bronzy-purple 'Advance' is one of the best known.

10cm / 8cm

CYCLAMEN HEDERIFOLIUM
CYCLAMEN
PRIMULACEAE

A tuberous perennial found in the Mediterranean, with clumps of heart-shaped mid- to dark green leaves. In mid- to late autumn, scented pink flowers are sometimes produced. A plant for a rock garden or for a raised bed. Grow in humus-rich, moderately fertile, moist but well-drained soil.

10cm / 10cm

CYRTANTHUS ELATUS
SCARBOROUGH LILY
AMARYLLIDACEAE

From South Africa's Western Cape, a deciduous perennial with erect leaves that produces funnel-shaped bright red flowers in late summer. A good plant for a windowbox or for the base of a sunny wall. Likes soil that is moderately fertile, humus-rich and well drained. Remember to plant deep.

60cm / 15cm

 height and spread   ✳ feature of interest   ▮▮▮ season of interest   *BULBS, CORMS AND TUBERS* **A – C**

BULBS, CORMS AND TUBERS

DAHLIA 'BISHOP OF LLANDAFF'
ASTERACEAE

Dahlias are half-hardy perennials growing from tuberous roots, with flowers in a wide range of forms and all colours, except a true blue, in late summer and autumn. 'Bishop of Llandaff' is a popular bedding variety with bronzy leaves and deep red, single flowers. Grow in soil that is fertile, humus-rich and well drained in full sunlight.

ERANTHIS HYEMALIS
WINTER ACONITE
RANUNCULACEAE

A perennial plant with tuberous roots, this winter aconite produces relatively large, buttercup-yellow, cup-shaped flowers backed by a green ruff of leafy bracts. These appear in late winter or early spring, with the deeply-cut, bronzy-green leaves dying down in summer. Grow in fertile, humus-rich soil.

ERYTHRONIUM DENS-CANIS
DOG'S TOOTH VIOLET
LILIACEAE

A hardy perennial, tuberous-rooted plant with long, pointed, oval leaves usually attractively mottled with purple and grey. In spring, each flowering stem carries a nodding, pink, white or lilac flower with lightly reflexing petals. Grow in fertile, humus-rich, well-drained soil.

FREESIA 'WHITE SWAN'
IRIDACEAE

A tender corm which produces erect, sword-shaped, light green leaves and spikes of funnel-shaped, very strongly fragrant white flowers. Numerous other varieties in various colours exist. In mild areas, plant corms outdoors in autumn; in cooler regions, special corms can be planted outdoors in spring for summer flowering. Grow in fertile, moist but well-drained soil.

FRITILLARIA MELEAGRIS
SNAKE'S HEAD FRITILLARY
LILIACEAE

A hardy, spring-flowering bulb with narrow, grey-green leaves and slender stems each bearing one or two gracefully pendent, lantern-shaped flowers. Notable for their unusual chequered pattern of white and purple or pink; several named varieties of different shades exist. Grow in fertile, moist soil.

GALANTHIS NIVALIS
COMMON SNOWDROP
AMARYLLIDACEAE

Hardy bulbs that are among the first flowers to signal the imminent arrival of spring. The strap-shaped leaves are blue-green; pendent white flowers then appear with green markings on the petals. Various named forms exist, including double varieties. Grow in humus-rich, moist but well-drained soil.

 leaf type   light preference   speed of growth   ease of growth

GLADIOLUS CALLIANTHUS 'MURIELIAE'

IRIDACEAE

A half-hardy corm which used to be known as *Acidanthera bicolor*. It produces erect, sword-shaped leaves and flowers in late summer – spikes of slightly nodding, fragrant, white-petalled blooms with deep purple markings at the centre. Plant in a sheltered spot in spring and lift the corms before the first frosts. Grow in fertile, well-drained soil.

1m / 15cm

IRIS HISTRIOIDES 'MAJOR'

IRIDACEAE

A tiny, bulbous iris producing narrow, deep green leaves and typical iris flowers in miniature; they are deep violet blue with yellow markings on the lower petals. Flowers are produced in early spring, while the leaves are just emerging. Suitable for rock gardens or shallow containers. Grow in well-drained, moderately fertile soil.

10cm / 5cm

LILIUM REGALE

LILY

LILIACEAE

Large, fleshy bulbs producing tall stems with linear leaves, crowned with a cluster of very showy, funnel-shaped, intensely fragrant flowers in summer. The flowers are white with golden centres and orange-gold anthers; the backs of the petals are dusky purple. Grow in well-drained, rich soil.

1.2m / 1.2m

NARCISSUS 'FEBRUARY GOLD'

DAFFODIL

AMARYLLIDACEAE

A hardy, spring-flowering bulb, 'February Gold' is one of many reliable varieties belonging to the Cyclamineus group of narcissus. It has golden flowers, which are perfect trumpet daffodils in miniature; they appear in early spring and are long lasting and weatherproof. Grow in fertile, well-drained soil.

25cm / 10cm

SCHIZOSTYLIS COCCINEA 'MAJOR'

KAFFIR LILY

IRIDACEAE

A hardy perennial growing from rhizomatous roots. The bright green foliage is narrow and forms a vigorous clump. Flower stems are produced in mid-autumn, bearing a spike of cup-shaped, silky-textured, deep crimson flowers. A valuable plant for late-season colour. Grow in fertile, moist, well-drained soil.

60cm / 30cm

TULIPA KAUFMANNIANA 'HEART'S DELIGHT'

TULIP

LILIACEAE

An early spring-flowering bulb. The long, broad, pointed leaves are grey-green, attractively mottled with brown. The petals of the cup-shaped flowers are red shading to rosy pink on the outside; inside they are pale pink with a yellow base blotched with red. Grow in fertile, well-drained soil.

200cm / 10cm

⬍ height and spread   ✳ feature of interest   ▮▮▮▮ season of interest   *BULBS, CORMS AND TUBERS* **D – T**

HERBACEOUS PERENNIALS

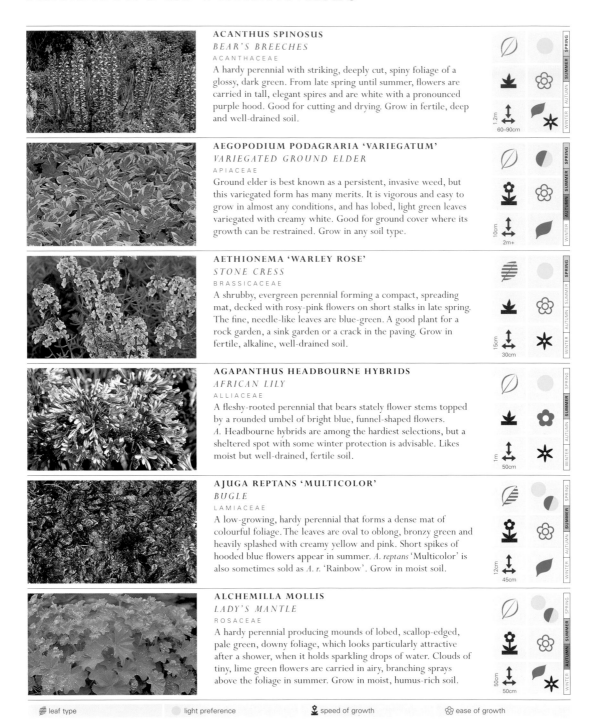

ACANTHUS SPINOSUS
BEAR'S BREECHES
ACANTHACEAE

A hardy perennial with striking, deeply cut, spiny foliage of a glossy, dark green. From late spring until summer, flowers are carried in tall, elegant spires and are white with a pronounced purple hood. Good for cutting and drying. Grow in fertile, deep and well-drained soil.

1.2m
60–90cm

AEGOPODIUM PODAGRARIA 'VARIEGATUM'
VARIEGATED GROUND ELDER
APIACEAE

Ground elder is best known as a persistent, invasive weed, but this variegated form has many merits. It is vigorous and easy to grow in almost any conditions, and has lobed, light green leaves variegated with creamy white. Good for ground cover where its growth can be restrained. Grow in any soil type.

10cm
2m+

AETHIONEMA 'WARLEY ROSE'
STONE CRESS
BRASSICACEAE

A shrubby, evergreen perennial forming a compact, spreading mat, decked with rosy-pink flowers on short stalks in late spring. The fine, needle-like leaves are blue-green. A good plant for a rock garden, a sink garden or a crack in the paving. Grow in fertile, alkaline, well-drained soil.

15cm
30cm

AGAPANTHUS HEADBOURNE HYBRIDS
AFRICAN LILY
ALLIACEAE

A fleshy-rooted perennial that bears stately flower stems topped by a rounded umbel of bright blue, funnel-shaped flowers. *A.* Headbourne hybrids are among the hardiest selections, but a sheltered spot with some winter protection is advisable. Likes moist but well-drained, fertile soil.

1m
50cm

AJUGA REPTANS 'MULTICOLOR'
BUGLE
LAMIACEAE

A low-growing, hardy perennial that forms a dense mat of colourful foliage. The leaves are oval to oblong, bronzy green and heavily splashed with creamy yellow and pink. Short spikes of hooded blue flowers appear in summer. *A. reptans* 'Multicolor' is also sometimes sold as *A. r.* 'Rainbow'. Grow in moist soil.

12cm
45cm

ALCHEMILLA MOLLIS
LADY'S MANTLE
ROSACEAE

A hardy perennial producing mounds of lobed, scallop-edged, pale green, downy foliage, which looks particularly attractive after a shower, when it holds sparkling drops of water. Clouds of tiny, lime green flowers are carried in airy, branching sprays above the foliage in summer. Grow in moist, humus-rich soil.

50cm
50cm

leaf type   light preference   speed of growth   ease of growth

ALSTROEMERIA HYBRIDS
PERUVIAN LILY
ALSTROEMERIACEAE

Derived mainly from crosses of *A. ligtu* and *A. haemantha*, these varieties are from a genus of plants originally from South America. Erect stems and linear, green leaves are joined in summer by funnel-shaped flowers in a range of colours. Good for a scree or for a border. Grow in moist, well-drained, fertile soil.

50cm / 75cm

AQUILEGIA FLABELLATA CAMEO SERIES
COLUMBINE, GRANNY'S BONNET
RANUNCULACEAE

Hardy perennial rock garden plants forming compact clumps of glaucous green, finely-divided leaves topped with nodding, bell-shaped, short-spurred flowers. Colours include white, blue with white, rose red with white and pink with white. Plants are often short lived. Grow in fertile, moist and well-drained soil.

25cm / 10cm

ARMERIA MARITIMA 'ALBA'
THRIFT
PLUMBAGINACEAE

A hardy perennial that forms neat cushions of deep green, needle-like foliage decked in summer with round, drumstick heads of long-lasting, papery, white flowers on slender but sturdy stems. The evergreen foliage remains attractive even when the flowers have finished. Grow in well-drained, poor soil.

10cm / 15cm

ASTER NOVI-BELGII
MICHAELMAS DAISY
ASTERACEAE

Hardy perennials with deep green, linear leaves and tall stems topped with heads of many daisy-like flowers in autumn. Colour range includes red, purple, blue, white and violet; flowers may be single, double or semi-double. Plants are prone to mildew in hot, dry summers. Likes fertile, moist soil.

0.5-1.2m / 90cm

ASTRANTIA MAJOR
GREATER MASTERWORT
APIACEAE

A hardy perennial with lobed, palmate leaves. The flowers, produced on branching, wiry stems in summer, consist of papery, greenish-white or pink-tinged, petal-like bracts, with a cluster of small, pink flowers in the centre, which look like pins sticking in a pink cushion. Likes moist, humus-rich soil.

60cm / 45cm

AUBRIETA 'DOCTOR MULES'
ROCK CRESS
BRASSICACEAE

A perennial trailer with grey-green, elongated oval leaves on stems, which form a spreading mat or trail over the edges of raised beds or the tops of walls. In spring the stems are closely covered with large, double, bright purple flowers, making a carpet of colour. Grow in fertile, well-drained soil.

8cm / 30cm

---

 height and spread   ✳ feature of interest   ▭▭▭ season of interest   *HERBACEOUS PERENNIALS* **A**

HERBACEOUS PERENNIALS

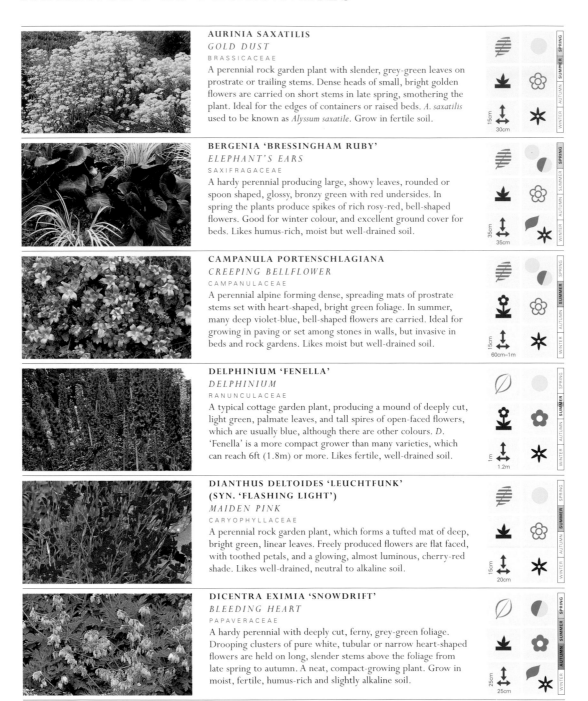

AURINIA SAXATILIS
GOLD DUST
BRASSICACEAE

A perennial rock garden plant with slender, grey-green leaves on prostrate or trailing stems. Dense heads of small, bright golden flowers are carried on short stems in late spring, smothering the plant. Ideal for the edges of containers or raised beds. *A. saxatilis* used to be known as *Alyssum saxatile*. Grow in fertile soil.

BERGENIA 'BRESSINGHAM RUBY'
ELEPHANT'S EARS
SAXIFRAGACEAE

A hardy perennial producing large, showy leaves, rounded or spoon shaped, glossy, bronzy green with red undersides. In spring the plants produce spikes of rich rosy-red, bell-shaped flowers. Good for winter colour, and excellent ground cover for beds. Likes humus-rich, moist but well-drained soil.

CAMPANULA PORTENSCHLAGIANA
CREEPING BELLFLOWER
CAMPANULACEAE

A perennial alpine forming dense, spreading mats of prostrate stems set with heart-shaped, bright green foliage. In summer, many deep violet-blue, bell-shaped flowers are carried. Ideal for growing in paving or set among stones in walls, but invasive in beds and rock gardens. Likes moist but well-drained soil.

DELPHINIUM 'FENELLA'
DELPHINIUM
RANUNCULACEAE

A typical cottage garden plant, producing a mound of deeply cut, light green, palmate leaves, and tall spires of open-faced flowers, which are usually blue, although there are other colours. *D. 'Fenella'* is a more compact grower than many varieties, which can reach 6ft (1.8m) or more. Likes fertile, well-drained soil.

DIANTHUS DELTOIDES 'LEUCHTFUNK' (SYN. 'FLASHING LIGHT')
MAIDEN PINK
CARYOPHYLLACEAE

A perennial rock garden plant, which forms a tufted mat of deep, bright green, linear leaves. Freely produced flowers are flat faced, with toothed petals, and a glowing, almost luminous, cherry-red shade. Likes well-drained, neutral to alkaline soil.

DICENTRA EXIMIA 'SNOWDRIFT'
BLEEDING HEART
PAPAVERACEAE

A hardy perennial with deeply cut, ferny, grey-green foliage. Drooping clusters of pure white, tubular or narrow heart-shaped flowers are held on long, slender stems above the foliage from late spring to autumn. A neat, compact-growing plant. Grow in moist, fertile, humus-rich and slightly alkaline soil.

 leaf type   light preference    speed of growth   ease of growth

DODECATHEON MEADIA 'ALBUM'
SHOOTING STAR
PRIMULACEAE

A hardy perennial forming rosettes of long, oval, mid-green leaves. In late spring, white flowers are carried on long stems; their dark centres are pointed and the petals strongly reflexed. The species has rosy-pink flowers. Plants die down after flowering. Grow in moist but well-drained soil.

25cm
20cm

ECHINOPS RITRO
GLOBE THISTLE
ASTERACEAE

A hardy perennial with grey-green, divided leaves, which look spiny but are not. In summer, spherical, steely blue flowerheads are carried on strong, silvery stems above the foliage, gradually opening into a mass of starry, tubular blue flowers. Grow in poor, well-drained soil.

1.2m
1m

ERIGERON 'ROSA JUWEL'
FLEABANE
ASTERACEAE

Produces a clump of elongated oval, mid-green leaves and, in summer, large quantities of cheerful, daisy-like flowers with many bright pink, narrow petals and a golden, central disc. Flowers are produced over a long period. This variety is sometimes labelled 'Pink Jewel'. Likes fertile, well-drained soil.

60cm
60cm

ERYSIMUM 'BOWLES' MAUVE'
PERENNIAL WALLFLOWER
BRASSICACEAE

A hardy or half-hardy, short-lived perennial, still sometimes known as *Cheiranthus*. The leaves are grey-green and slender, on bushy stems, and elongated heads of deep pink, four-petalled flowers are carried in spring and early summer. Needs a sheltered position and poor, well-drained and ideally alkaline soil.

60cm
45cm

EUPHORBIA AMYGDALOIDES 'PURPUREA'
PURPLE WOOD SPURGE
EUPHORBIACEAE

In spring the stems and leaves are deep purple, the young shoot tips red; as the season progresses, the stems becomes deep maroon and the leaves a dark, purple-green. Acid-yellow flowerheads are carried in spring. *E. a.* 'Purpurea' is sometimes sold as *E. a.* 'Rubra'. Grow in moist, humus-rich soil.

30cm
30cm

GENTIANA ACAULIS
TRUMPET GENTIAN
GENTIANACEAE

Low, spreading growth with narrow, deep green leaves. In spring, and occasionally in autumn, it produces large, trumpet-shaped flowers on short stems; they are an intense, deep violet-blue. Sometimes difficult to bring into flower. This species was known as *G. kochiana*. Grow in light, moist but well-drained soil.

1cm
30cm

---

 height and spread   ✳ feature of interest    season of interest   *HERBACEOUS PERENNIALS **A – G***

HERBACEOUS PERENNIALS

GERANIUM 'JOHNSON'S BLUE'
CRANESBILL
GERANIACEAE

A hardy, tolerant perennial forming a mounded clump of light green, downy, much divided leaves. Saucer-shaped, lavender-blue flowers are carried in groups on slender stems just above the foliage; a long succession of blooms continues throughout the summer. Grow in fertile, well-drained soil.

GLECHOMA HEDERACEA 'VARIEGATA'
VARIEGATED GROUND IVY
LAMIACEAE

An evergreen or semi-evergreen perennial with kidney-shaped leaves produced on trailing stems. In summer, it produces whorls of lilac-mauve flowers. Because of its particularly beautiful foliage, this plant is often used in window boxes or hanging baskets. Grow in moderately fertile, moist but well-drained soil.

GYPSOPHILA PANICULATA
BABY'S BREATH
CARYOPHYLLACEAE

A hardy perennial plant which is valuable for the lacy, fluffy texture it provides in the garden. The leaves are linear and mid-green; slender, wiry, much-branched flower stems carry airy clouds of tiny white flowers in summer, which are excellent for cutting. Prefers chalky soils.

HELLEBORUS ARGUTIFOLIUS
CORSICAN HELLEBORE
RANUNCULACEAE

A shade-tolerant hardy perennial, also known as *H. corsicus*, that forms mounds of striking, deeply divided, spiny margined, dark green leaves; in late winter and spring, heavy clusters of pale green, cup-shaped flowers are carried on stout stems above the foliage. Likes neutral to alkaline soil.

HELLEBORUS NIGER
CHRISTMAS ROSE
RANUNCULACEAE

A hardy perennial with dark green, divided leaves and relatively large, nodding, saucer-shaped white flowers with gold stamens. These are produced in winter or (more commonly) early spring, and should be protected from mud splashes from the soil, which often spoil them in rainy weather. Likes neutral to alkaline soil.

HEUCHERA MICRANTHA VAR. DIVERSIFOLIA 'PALACE PURPLE'
CORAL FLOWER
SAXIFRAGACEAE

A hardy perennial with lobed, shiny, deep purple-maroon leaves which hold their colour well throughout the season. In summer, airy sprays of small, white, tubular flowers are carried on slender stems above the foliage. Likes fertile, moist and neutral soil.

leaf type   light preference   speed of growth   ease of growth

HOSTA 'GINKO CRAIG'
PLANTAIN LILY
HOSTACEAE

A hardy perennial with showy, lance-shaped, strongly veined leaves of mid-green with fine white margins; a neat and compact grower, suitable for small spaces. Spikes of bell-shaped, lilac flowers are produced in summer. All varieties are very prone to slug and snail damage. Grow in fertile, moist, well-drained soil.

30cm ↕ 45cm

IBERIS SEMPERVIRENS
CANDYTUFT
BRASSICACEAE

A low-growing, spreading sub-shrub with slender, deep green leaves and domed, rounded heads of white flowers in spring and early summer. Many clusters of flowers are carried, usually completely smothering the plant. Good for the edges of raised beds and walls. Likes poor, moist, neutral to alkaline soil.

23cm ↕ 60cm

KNIPHOFIA 'LITTLE MAID'
RED HOT POKER
ASPHODELACEAE

A hardy perennial producing a spreading clump of grassy, dark green foliage. In summer, the compact 'Little Maid' produces upright stems closely clustered with creamy yellow, tubular flowers. Traditional varieties, which are taller, have glowing orange flower spikes, hence the name. Grow in deep, fertile soil.

60cm ↕ 45cm

LAMIUM MACULATUM 'GOLDEN ANNIVERSARY'
DEAD NETTLE
LAMIACEAE

A hardy perennial often treated as an annual; it is a popular foliage plant for containers and hanging baskets. Toothed, heart shaped leaves are typically nettle-like, but are light green, with a broad golden margin and a pronounced silvery streak down the centre of each leaf. Likes any soil, but less vigorous in poor soil.

25cm ↕ 1m

LEONTOPODIUM ALPINUM
EDELWEISS
ASTERACEAE

Low tufts of lance-shaped, hairy, mid-green leaves and small, white, insignificant flowers in early summer, surrounded by showy, felted, silvery bracts which look like long, narrow petals. The plant tends to be short-lived, and must be protected from damp conditions. Likes sharply drained, slightly alkaline soil.

15cm ↕ 20cm

LEWISIA COTYLEDON SUNSET GROUP
LEWISIA
PORTULACACEAE

Forms rosettes of long, spoon-shaped, dark green, fleshy leaves, and, in late spring or early summer, flowering stems bear clusters of very showy, cup-shaped flowers in a range of beautiful, glowing colours. Dislikes damp conditions. Grow in sharply drained, neutral to acid, fertile soil.

30cm ↕ 23cm

HERBACEOUS PERENNIALS

LITHODORA DIFFUSA 'HEAVENLY BLUE'
BORAGINACEAE

A hardy sub-shrub forming a spreading mat of deep green, lance-shaped leaves on prostrate stems. In summer, the plant is heavily sprinkled with brilliant gentian-blue, funnel-shaped flowers. A good choice for a rock garden or edge of a raised bed, though it can sometimes be difficult to establish. Likes well-drained, fertile, acid soil.

LYSIMACHIA NUMMULARIA 'AUREA'
GOLDEN CREEPING JENNY
PRIMULACEAE

A hardy, herbaceous perennial with creeping, prostrate stems. The leaves, which are carried in opposite pairs, are round, like coins, and a soft yellow or lime-green shade. Buttercup-yellow, cup-shaped flowers appear in summer. Adaptable to a wide range of conditions. Grow in humus-rich, moist soil.

MONARDA 'BEAUTY OF COBHAM'
BERGAMOT
LAMIACEAE

A hardy perennial with mid-green, lanceolate, aromatic leaves and shaggy heads of hooded, pink flowers in whorls. The flowers are very popular with bees and butterflies; the leaves can be dried for use in pot pourri or to make a citrus-scented tisane. Grow in fertile, moist but well-drained, humus-rich soil.

OENOTHERA FRUTICOSA 'FYRVERKERI'
(SYN. 'FIREWORKS')
SUNDROPS
ONAGACEAE

Has slender, lanceolate, mid-green leaves and tall, red-tinged stems bearing clusters of golden-yellow, cup-shaped flowers that open from tightly scrolled buds. Flowers from midsummer to early autumn. Likes fertile, well-drained soil.

OPHIOPOGON PLANISCAPUS 'NIGRESCENS'
LILYTURF
CONVALLARIACEAE

A hardy perennial plant with unusual, grassy foliage which is a deep, purplish black, making an effective contrast with lighter-leaved subjects. In summer it bears clusters of pale violet flowers, which are followed by black fruits. Best in well-drained and sandy soil.

PAEONIA LACTIFLORA 'SARAH BERNHARDT'
PEONY
PAEONIACEAE

A hardy perennial plant that produces bold, deeply cut foliage late in the spring, and carries very large, showy flowerheads in late spring and early summer. *P.* 'Sarah Bernhardt' is fully double, silvery pink and sweetly scented. Flowers are easily spoiled by bad weather. Grow in deep, fertile, humus-rich soil.

leaf type   light preference   speed of growth   ease of growth

PRIMULA 'SUE JERVIS'
DOUBLE PRIMROSE
PRIMULACEAE

A hardy perennial producing a rosette of tongue-shaped, wrinkled, bright green leaves. In spring, bears fully double, buff-pink flowers, which look rather like miniature roses. 'Sue Jervis' is one of several double-flowered varieties in a range of colours now freely available. Likes humus-rich, fertile, well-drained soil.

SAXIFRAGA X ELISABETHAE
SAXIFRAGE
SAXIFRAGACEAE

A hardy, low-growing perennial with narrow, deep green, spiny leaves forming a tight cushion of foliage. In spring, primrose yellow, open-faced flowers are carried in profusion on slender, red-tinted stems. Great in a rock garden setting. Likes moist but well-drained soil.

SEDUM KAMTSCHATICUM VAR. FLORIFERUM 'WEIHENSTEPHANER GOLD'
STONECROP
CRASSULACEAE

In summer, the foliage is covered with clusters of star-shaped, golden-orange flowers with prominent stamens, carried on dark red stems. Attractive foliage colours well in autumn. Likes neutral to alkaline, fertile and well-drained soil.

SEMPERVIVUM ARACHNOIDEUM
COBWEB HOUSELEEK
CRASSULACEAE

Produces dense rosettes of succulent, pointed leaves which may be tinted red, especially in cool or dry conditions. The tips are spun together with fine, white threads like a spider's web, giving a silver, woolly appearance. In summer, thick red stems bear clusters of rosy-red flowers. Likes poor, gritty, well-drained soil.

STACHYS BYZANTINA 'SILVER CARPET'
LAMB'S TONGUE
LAMIACEAE

Forms a spreading mat of oval leaves densely covered with glistening grey hairs with a soft, furry texture. It makes an excellent ground-cover plant. *S. b.* 'Silver Carpet' is a non-flowering variety, though an occasional spike of lilac flowers may be produced. Grow in well-drained, moderately fertile soil.

VIOLA 'MOLLY SANDERSON'
PANSY
VIOLACEAE

A hardy perennial forming neat clumps of oval or heart shaped, mid-green leaves. The small, pansy-shaped flowers are an intensely dark purple-black with a small golden eye, and very freely produced. Plants are short lived. They make good edging or container subjects. Likes fertile, moist but well-drained soil.

 height and spread   ✳ feature of interest   ▮ season of interest   *HERBACEOUS PERENNIALS* **L – V**

GRASSES, BAMBOOS AND FERNS

BRIZA MAXIMA
QUAKING GRASS
POACEAE

An annual grass forming a compact tuft of narrow, bright green leaves. The slender flowering stems carry loose panicles of pendent spikelets, which are pale green tinged with purple. The flower stems dry well for use in flower arrangements; when left in place, they will often self-seed freely. Likes well-drained soil.

FESTUCA GLAUCA
BLUE FESCUE
POACEAE

A hardy perennial grass that makes a neat tuft of narrow leaves, which are a striking blue-grey. Their colour is especially strong in summer, when they also carry feathery cream flower spikelets above the foliage. Several named varieties of various intensities of colour exist. Grow in poor, dry, well-drained soil.

HAKONECHLOA MACRA 'AUREOLA'
POACEAE

A hardy perennial grass with slender, green and gold striped leaves which form a spreading, arching clump to give the impression of a fountain of foliage. On established plants, red-tinted flower spikes may appear in autumn. An excellent specimen plant for a container. Grow in a fertile, moist but well-drained and humus-rich soil.

PENNISETUM ALOPECUROIDES
CHINESE FOUNTAIN GRASS
POACEAE

A hardy perennial grass with narrow, greyish leaves forming a compact, arching clump. In midsummer, flowerheads appear, with feathery, rusty-brown plumes which become tinged with purple in autumn, persisting into the winter. Grow in very well-drained, fertile soil.

PLEIOBLASTUS VARIEGATUS (SYN. ARUNDINARIA FORTUNEI)
DWARF BAMBOO
POACEAE

A hardy perennial bamboo with narrow, dark green leaves attractively striped with white and pale green. It is not as invasive as some bamboos, but still spreads quite quickly. A good choice for a container. Grow in moist, fertile, humus-rich soil.

POLYSTICHUM POLYBLEPHARUM
JAPANESE TASSEL FERN
DRYOPTERIDACEAE

A hardy perennial fern of graceful form, with broad, arching fronds of mid-green on dark stalks. In winter, the finely cut foliage is tinged with bronzy purple. Like many ferns, it is a reliable plant for a shaded situation. Grow in fertile, well-drained, humus-rich soil.

 leaf type   light preference    speed of growth   ease of growth

CONIFERS

ABIES BALSAMEA – HUDSONIA GROUP
BALSAM FIR

PINACEAE

A dwarf conifer forming a rounded, compact bush which will take many years to reach the eventual height and spread shown. The needles are densely set, and are glossy mid-green above and silver on their undersides; they have an aromatic, balsam scent when crushed. Grow in fertile, slightly acid soil.

60cm / 1m

CHAMAECYPARIS PISIFERA 'BOULEVARD'
SAWARA CYPRESS

CUPRESSACEAE

A conifer with bright steely-blue foliage that is soft to the touch and feathery in appearance. 'Boulevard' eventually forms a medium-sized, conical tree but remains suitable for small gardens for many years. Keep moist and protected from cold winds. Grow in fertile, well-drained soil.

2m / 1m

JUNIPERUS SCOPULORUM 'SKYROCKET'
ROCKY MOUNTAIN JUNIPER

CUPRESSACEAE

A popular dwarf conifer making a very narrow, upright, columnar plant with soft, blue-green foliage. It is frequently used in rock gardens and to give height among a planting of heathers. Although it can eventually become a tall tree, it will take several years to do so. Grow in well-drained soil.

2.5m+ / 60cm

PICEA PUNGENS 'GLOBOSA'
COLORADO SPRUCE

PINACEAE

A dwarf conifer with very dense, bushy growth and attractive, silver-blue foliage in the form of stiff, bristly needles set all round the branches. It makes a rounded, dumpy, rather flat-topped bush. Foliage colour is at its brightest in early summer. Grow in deep, moist, neutral to acid soil.

60cm / 60cm

PINUS MUGO 'MOPS'
DWARF MOUNTAIN PINE

PINACEAE

A very hardy dwarf conifer that forms a dense, spherical bush with long, dark green needles carried in pairs. It is tolerant of most soil types, including very poor soils. 'Mops' is just one of a number of dwarf forms of the mountain pine. Grow in well-drained soil.

1m / 1m

TAXUS BACCATA 'STANDISHII'
YEW

TAXACEAE

A hardy conifer with linear, needly leaves of a glowing, muted gold shade, densely packed all round the stems. It grows very slowly, making a strongly upright, narrow column. The seeds within the bright red, fleshy, berry-like fruits, and all other parts of the tree, are poisonous. Grow in any well-drained, fertile soil.

1.2m / 60cm

---

 height and spread   ✳ feature of interest   ▭ season of interest   *GRASSES AND CONIFERS*

CLIMBERS

CLEMATIS 'ERNEST MARKHAM'

RANUNCULACEAE

A popular perennial climber with toothed, mid-green leaves divided into three leaflets, and large, open-faced flowers of a glowing rosy magenta. Flowers are produced in late summer, on the current season's growth. Provide a sturdy support for the plant to twine round. Grow in fertile, well-drained soil.

ECCREMOCARPUS SCABER 'AUREUS'

CHILEAN GLORY FLOWER

BIGNONIACEAE

A perennial climber often grown as an annual. The dark green leaves are divided into a number of leaflets which end in coiling tendrils. Long racemes of yellow, tubular flowers are carried through the summer and into autumn; red and orange forms are also available. Grow in fertile, well-drained soil.

HEDERA HELIX 'ORO DI BOGLIASCO' (SYN. 'GOLDHEART')

SMALL-LEAVED IVY

ARALIACEAE

A hardy, vigorous climber, ivy is one of the most versatile garden plants. The leaves are characteristically lobed; this variety is dark, glossy green with a bright, gold-splashed centre. The woody stems are self-clinging, with aerial roots. Tolerates most soils.

HUMULUS LUPULUS 'AUREUS'

GOLDEN HOP

CANNABACEAE

The leaves of 'Aureus' are a soft, glowing yellow-green shade. Vigorous, strongly twining stems scramble over any suitable support. Green, papery, hop flowers are carried in dangling clusters in late summer on established plants. Likes moist, well-drained, fertile soil.

JASMINUM OFFICINALE

JASMINE

OLEACEAE

A woody-stemmed, twining climber that likes a sheltered spot. The leaves are deep green and rather ferny, being composed of a number of leaflets. In summer, clusters of pure white flowers are produced; they are tubular, opening to a star shape, and are heavily scented. Grow in fertile, well-drained soil.

LONICERA PERICLYMENUM 'SEROTINA'

HONEYSUCKLE

CAPRIFOLIACEAE

A hardy, woody-stemmed climber with ovate, mid-green, greyish leaves. The flowers are tubular with protruding stamens, purple-red outside and white within; they are very strongly and sweetly scented and are carried from midsummer until autumn. Grow in fertile, moist but well-drained, humus-rich soil.

≋ leaf type   ● light preference   ⚘ speed of growth   ✿ ease of growth

PARTHENOCISSUS HENRYANA
CHINESE VIRGINIA CREEPER
VITACEAE

A moderately hardy, woody-stemmed climber with leaves divided into three or five leaflets of a bronzy grey-green (orange-red in autumn) with the veins picked out in silvery pink. Needs a sheltered position to become established. Leaf colour is best out of full sun. Will do well in any fertile, well-drained soil.

6m / 3m

PASSIFLORA CAERULEA
PASSION FLOWER
PASSIFLORACEAE

Has attractive, dark green foliage and striking flowers in summer. The spreading petals and sepals are white, and behind prominent stamens is a fringe-like corona of fine, blue and white filaments. In warm weather, orange, egg-shaped fruits follow. Needs a sheltered position and fertile, moist but well-drained soil.

5m / 3m

SOLANUM CRISPUM 'GLASNEVIN'
CHILEAN POTATO TREE
SOLANACEAE

A moderately hardy wall shrub used as a climber that has light green, softly downy, oval leaves on scrambling stems. In summer it carries clusters of purple, star-shaped flowers with prominent golden anthers – very similar to potato flowers in appearance. Grow in fertile, well-drained, slightly alkaline soil.

4.5m / 2.4m

TROPAEOLUM SPECIOSUM
FLAME CREEPER
TROPAEOLACEAE

An elegant perennial climber with long, thin rhizomes and palmate green leaves. Between summer and autumn, the plant produces bright red to crimson flowers with clawed petals. These are superseded by blue fruit. Grow in soil that is moist but well drained, and moderately fertile.

3m+ / 1m

VITIS COIGNETIAE
CRIMSON GLORY VINE
VITACEAE

A vigorous climber with large, lobed or heart-shaped leaves which are mid-green and veined, with reddish-brown hairs on the undersides. In autumn they turn spectacular shades of orange, yellow and crimson. The plant bears small, inedible, purple-black grapes. Grow in well-drained, neutral to alkaline soil.

6m+ / 3m+

WISTERIA SINENSIS
CHINESE WISTERIA
PAPILIONACEAE

Pinnate leaves produced on twining, woody stems. The flowers are carried in early summer, usually before the leaves are fully open – long, trailing racemes of scented, lilac blooms. Good against a sheltered wall, or can be trained as a standard in a tub. Choose fertile, moist but well-drained soil.

6m+ / 2.4m

---

 height and spread   ✳ feature of interest   ▮▮▮ season of interest   *CLIMBERS* **C – W**

TENDER SHRUBS AND PERENNIALS

AGAVE AMERICANA 'MEDIOPICTA'
CENTURY PLANT
AGAVACEAE

A succulent half-hardy perennial that needs a frost-free place to overwinter. The fleshy, sword-shaped leaves form a large rosette, and are sharply toothed, with yellow stripes along their centre; the tips of the leaves usually curve outwards. A good architectural plant. Grow in slightly acid, well-drained soil.

ANISODONTEA CAPENSIS
MALVACEAE

A perennial shrub that is not frost hardy, so needs winter protection. The oval leaves are deeply lobed; bowl-shaped, rose-magenta flowers are freely produced in summer. It can be successfully trained as a standard. Good in soil that is deep, moist but well drained and fertile, and best in full sun.

ARGYRANTHEMUM FRUTESCENS 'SHARPITOR'
MARGUERITE
ASTERACEAE

Tender perennial with rich green, lobed and divided, aromatic leaves and a profusion of daisy-like flowers — white-petalled with yellow centres in the species; cultivars may have pink or yellow, single or double blooms. Ideal for training as a standard. Grow in well-drained, fertile soil.

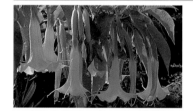

BRUGMANSIA X CANDIDA 'GRAND MARNIER'
ANGEL'S TRUMPETS
SOLANACEAE

A tender shrub previously known as *Datura*, with long, green leaves and large, trumpet-shaped, peach-coloured flowers in summer. All parts of the plant are poisonous. Needs a sheltered position and must be taken under cover in winter. Whitefly may be a problem. Grow in fertile, moist but well-drained soil.

X CITROFORTUNELLA MICROCARPA
CALAMONDIN
RUTACEAE

A hybrid between a tangerine and a kumquat, this plant is best known as a house plant, but can make an exotic patio plant in a warm, sheltered position. The leaves are aromatic when crushed. Fragrant white flowers are followed by small orange fruits which can be used for preserves. Grow in neutral to acid, loamy soil.

CLIANTHUS PUNICEUS
PARROT'S BILL
PAPILIONACEAE

An exotic-looking, woody, scrambling climber that needs a warm and sheltered position against a wall. The pinnate leaves are attractively ferny; bright scarlet, claw-shaped summer flowers are carried in clusters in the leaf axils. Overwinter under cover in cold areas. Grow in well-drained soil.

 leaf type　　　　light preference　　　　🌱 speed of growth　　　　ease of growth

CORDYLINE AUSTRALIS 'TORBAY DAZZLER'
NEW ZEALAND CABBAGE PALM
AGAVACEAE

A half-hardy shrub that will form a tree in mild locations, but is generally grown as a smaller container plant. Stiff, sword-like leaves are mid-green, boldly striped at the edges with yellow. They are carried in a striking rosette which, after a year or two, tops a stout trunk. Grow in fertile, well-drained soil.

2m / 90cm

DICKSONIA ANTARCTICA
AUSTRALIAN TREE FERN
DICKSONIACEAE

Evergreen fern of tree-like proportions, with a stout trunk topped with a spreading rosette of large, finely divided fronds In spring, new fronds arise from the centre as showy, tightly curled spirals on long stems. A striking (if expensive) specimen plant for a warm, sheltered garden. Grow in acid, humus-rich soil.

3m / 1.8m+

FUCHSIA 'DOLLAR PRINCESS'
FUCHSIA
ONAGRACEAE

A bushy, moderately hardy variety with red sepals and violet-blue petals, making 'Dollar Princess' excellent for containers. Trailing varieties such as 'Swingtime' are particularly good for hanging baskets. Needs soil that is moist, fertile and well drained, and needs shelter from harsh winds.

1m / 50cm

LANTANA CAMARA
YELLOW SAGE
VERBENACEAE

Deep green, oval, wrinkled leaves are joined by fragrant, tubular flowers borne in rounded heads. Flowers start off cream or pink, gradually turning yellow then deep orange as they age, so all three colours can be found on the same flowerhead at one time. Grow in fertile, moist but well-drained soil.

1m / 1.2m

TECOMA CAPENSIS
CAPE HONEYSUCKLE
BIGNONIACEAE

A tender, bushy, climbing shrub with attractively ferny, bright green leaves divided into leaflets. The tubular, honeysuckle-like flowers carried in short spikes in summer may be orange, red, yellow or apricot in colour; separate colour selections are usually available. Provide support and moist, well-drained, fertile soil.

2m / 1m

ZANTEDESCHIA ELLIOTTIANA
GOLDEN ARUM
ARACEAE

A tender, tuberous-rooted perennial with large, heart-shaped leaves that are marked with silvery, transparent streaks and spots. In early summer, the arum-like flowers are borne, consisting of a golden-yellow spathe wrapped around a central yellow spadix. Grow in moist, humus-rich soil.

75cm / 60cm

---

 height and spread   ✳ feature of interest   ▮▮▮▮ season of interest   *SHRUBS AND PERENNIALS **A – Z***

TREES AND SHRUBS

ABUTILON X SUNTENSE
ABUTILON
MALVACEAE

A vigorous upright shrub with narrow, ovate, grey-green, toothed leaves. During late spring and early summer, the plant produces saucer-shaped, white to purple flowers on tall stems. Good as a house plant or for a sheltered area. Grow in soil that is well-drained and moderately fertile.

ACER PALMATUM – DISSECTUM ATROPURPUREUM GROUP
JAPANESE MAPLE
ACERACEAE

An attractive small tree with finely divided, rich bronzy-red foliage which colours well in autumn. It is ideal for a tub. Shelter from cold winds. There are lots of other suitable *A. palmatum* varieties. Grow in moist but well-drained, fertile soil.

AESCULUS PAVIA
RED BUCKEYE
HIPPOCASTANACEAE

A shrub or small tree with mid-green leaves, which are an ovate shape. Flowers are borne in panicles, and are red, occasionally flecked with yellow. These are followed by attractive, smooth-skinned fruit which will cause stomach ache if eaten. Grow in fertile, moist but well-drained soil.

ALOYSIA TRIPHYLLA
LEMON VERBENA
VERBENACEAE

A bushy shrub with an upright nature and lemon-scented, bright green leaves. In late summer, it produces tiny lilac or white flowers on slender panicles. Good at the base of a sunny wall. Grow in soil that is well drained, poor and dry. Leaves can be used to make pot pourri.

ARBUTUS UNEDO
STRAWBERRY TREE
ERICACEAE

A small tree that is native to the Republic of Ireland. It has glossy, glaucous green leaves and white flowers in early summer, superseded by orangey fruit. Good for a border or as a specimen plant. Grow in humus-rich, fertile, moist but well-drained soil.

ARTEMISIA 'POWIS CASTLE'
WORMWOOD
ASTERACEAE

A moderately hardy shrub with finely divided, fern-like, bright silver-grey foliage. Sprays of dull grey summer flowers are usually removed to prevent them detracting from the foliage effect. Cut the stems back hard in early spring for vigorous new growth. Grow in well-drained, fertile soil.

🍃 leaf type   ● light preference   ⚘ speed of growth   ❁ ease of growth

AUCUBA JAPONICA 'GOLD DUST'
SPOTTED LAUREL
CORNACEAE

A vigorous, tolerant shrub with leathery, green leaves spotted and sprinkled with yellow. 'Gold Dust' will carry red berries if there is a male plant nearby for pollination. Young plants can be used as temporary winter residents for windowboxes; in a tub they will grow to medium-sized shrubs. Grow in any soil.

BERBERIS THUNBERGII 'ATROPURPUREA NANA'
BARBERRY
BERBERIDACEAE

A dwarf shrub with slightly arching, spiny branches clothed with bronzy-purple leaves which turn brilliant red in autumn. Produces yellow flowers in mid-spring, followed by small red fruit. Very compact and suitable for the smallest garden. Grow in well-drained soil.

BETULA PENDULA 'YOUNGII'
YOUNG'S WEEPING BIRCH
BETULACEAE

A small tree with a strongly weeping habit, forming a distinctive dome shape. The trunk develops attractive white bark as it ages. A good specimen tree, which casts only light, dappled shade: the slender, weeping branches make a pleasing outline in winter. Grow in moist but well-drained, moderately fertile soil.

BUDDLEJA DAVIDII 'ROYAL RED'
BUTTERFLY BUSH
BUDDLEJACEAE

A fast-growing, tolerant shrub that produces coarse, lance-shaped, mid-green leaves on arching branches, which, during the summer, bear long plumes of honey-scented flowers at their tips. 'Royal Red' is a glowing magenta. All attract butterflies. Prune stems down hard in early spring. Likes any well-drained soil.

BUXUS SEMPERVIRENS
COMMON BOX
BUXACEAE

An evergreen shrub that has small, oval, deep green, glossy leaves. Box grows slowly and with a compact habit. It responds well to clipping, making it a very popular subject for topiary and low hedges. It tolerates shade well. Grow in fertile, well-drained soil.

CALLUNA VULGARIS 'SPRING CREAM'
HEATHER
ERICACEAE

One of the many varieties of heather available, all hardy, bushy, low-growing shrubs with fine, needle-like foliage. 'Spring Cream' looks particularly attractive in spring, when the new growth at the tips of the shoots is a striking creamy colour. In autumn, the plant bears white flowers. Grow in well-drained, acid soil.

---

 height and spread   ✳ feature of interest   ▮▮ season of interest   *TREES AND SHRUBS* **A – C**

TREES AND SHRUBS

CAMELLIA RUSTICANA 'ARAJISHI'
CAMELLIA
THEACEAE
This cultivar has rosy-red, peony-type flowers. More common are forms of *Camellia japonica*, which has single, semi-double or double-flowered forms in white, pink or red. Flowers appear very early in spring; a sheltered position is necessary to avoid frost damage. Grow in moist, humus-rich, acid soil.

CARAGANA ARBORESCENS
PEA TREE
PAPILIONACEAE
Originally from Russia and parts of China, this thorny tree has light green leaves and, in late spring, clusters of pale yellow flowers. When flowers die down, small brown pods appear. Grow in soil that is well drained and moderately fertile.

CEANOTHUS THYRSIFLORUS VAR. REPENS
CREEPING BLUE BLOSSOM
RHAMNACEAE
A hardy, low-growing shrub, which forms a dense mound of small, shiny, dark green leaves. In early summer, it is thickly covered with panicles of powder-blue blossoms. One of the hardiest evergreen *Ceanothus*, it nevertheless will do best in a sheltered position. Grow in fertile, well-drained soil.

CHAENOMELES X SUPERBA
JAPANESE QUINCE
ROSACEAE
A hardy, thorny shrub best grown against a wall. It bears numerous red or pink, cup-shaped flowers in very early spring – as the fresh green leaves are unfurling, or even while the branches are still bare. Flowers are followed by round, yellow, aromatic fruits. Grow in well-drained, moderately fertile soil.

CHIMONANTHUS PRAECOX
WINTERSWEET
CALYCANTHACEAE
A deciduous, bushy shrub that carries its cup-shaped flowers on bare branches in winter. The blooms are a bright, clear yellow with purple centres, and very fragrant, with a strong, spicy scent. They appear sporadically in mild spells throughout the winter months. Grow in fertile, well-drained soil.

CHOISYA TERNATA
MEXICAN ORANGE BLOSSOM
RUTACEAE
A hardy, rounded shrub with fresh green, shiny leaves divided into three leaflets; they are sharply aromatic when crushed. In spring, waxy white, sweet-scented flowers like orange blossoms appear in clusters towards the ends of the shoots. Does best in a sheltered spot. Grow in fertile, well-drained soil.

---

 leaf type   ● light preference   ♨ speed of growth   ✿ ease of growth

CISTUS 'SILVER PINK'
SUN ROSE
CISTACEAE

A low-growing, bushy shrub with lance-shaped, silvery green leaves on spreading stems, and large, saucer-shaped, clear pink flowers in summer, each of which has a conspicuous bunch of bright golden stamens. Free flowering. Grow in poor to moderate, well-drained soil.

CONVOLVULUS CNEORUM
CONVOLVULACEAE

A compact, bushy shrub with silver-green, silky leaves. From late spring to summer, the plant bears attractive, funnel-shaped white flowers, which have yellow centres. Good for a rock garden. Grow in soil which is poor to moderate, well drained and even slightly gritty.

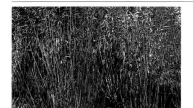

CORNUS ALBA 'SIBIRICA'
RED-BARKED DOGWOOD
CORNACEAE

A vigorous shrub grown mainly for its shining crimson winter stems. The oval leaves are mid-green, turning orange in autumn; in summer there are flattened heads of creamy-white flowers. In spring, prune back to within a few centimetres of the ground. Grow in fertile, moist, even wet, soil.

CORYLUS AVELLANA 'CONTORTA'
CORKSCREW HAZEL
CORYLACEAE

Its strangely spiralled, twisted and corkscrewed branches make a very decorative outline during the winter months, particularly when they are hung with pale golden catkins. Any straight branches should be pruned out at their base as soon as they appear. Grow in fertile, well-drained soil. Good in chalky soils.

COTONEASTER SALICIFOLIUS 'PENDULUS'
ROSACEAE

A hardy arching shrub that is virtually always grown as a weeping standard, grafted on to an upright stem. The leaves are small, oval and dark, glossy green; small, white summer flowers are followed by pea-sized, brilliant red fruits which last well if they are protected from birds. Grow in well-drained, moderately fertile soil.

CYTISUS BATTANDIERI
PINEAPPLE BROOM
PAPILIONACEAE

An upright-growing shrub with attractive leaves that are covered with silvery hairs. In early summer, dense racemes of golden-yellow, pineapple-scented flowers are freely produced. Needs a sheltered spot in cold areas, but can make a large bush where it is happy. Grow in fertile, well-drained soil.

---

 height and spread    feature of interest   season of interest   *TREES AND SHRUBS* **C**

TREES AND SHRUBS

DAPHNE ODORA 'AUREOMARGINATA'
DAPHNE
THYMELAEACEAE

A hardy shrub with pointed, inversely lance-shaped or oval leaves which have a very narrow, cream margin. In winter, pale lilac, tubular flowers open from purple-pink buds and carry a very strong, sweet fragrance. 'Aureomarginata' is a hardier form than the species. Thrives in well-drained soil.

1.5m / 1.5m

DEUTZIA GRACILIS
DEUTZIA
HYDRANGEACEAE

A bushy shrub with an airy, delicate appearance. The toothed, lance-shaped to ovate, elegantly tapered leaves are bright green, and the pure white, star-shaped flowers are carried in great profusion from spring to early summer, sometimes almost smothering the plant. Grow in fertile soil that is not too dry.

1.2m / 1.2m

ELAEAGNUS PUNGENS 'MACULATA'
ELAEAGNUS
ELAEAGNACEAE

A hardy, branching, bright and colourful shrub whose leathery, oval leaves are deep, glossy green with a broad golden splash in the centre. In autumn it carries bell-shaped white flowers with a strong, sweet scent, followed by scaly, red fruit. Requires fertile, well-drained soil.

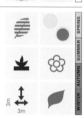

3m / 3m

ERICA CARNEA 'MYRETOUN RUBY'
WINTER-FLOWERING HEATH
ERICACEAE

A sub-shrub producing low, spreading growth, its stems set with deep green, needle-like, linear leaves. In late winter and early spring, spikes of rich reddish-purple, bell-like flowers that deepen with age are carried. More tolerant of chalky soils than many other *Erica* species, but ideal soil is well-drained and acid.

20cm / 30cm

ESCALLONIA 'APPLE BLOSSOM'
ESCALLONIA
ESCALLONIACEAE

Slightly tender shrub which thrives in mild areas but likes a sheltered spot in cold regions. Dense, bushy growth, with oval, toothed leaves of a fresh, glossy, bright green. Open-faced, tubular flowers, carried in profusion throughout the summer, are a delicate shell-pink. Grow in fertile, well-drained soil.

1.5m / 1.5m

EUCALYPTUS GUNNII
CIDER GUM
MYRTACEAE

Tree native to Australia, with attractive, aromatic foliage and bark. The round, juvenile leaves are bright, steely blue, giving way to lance-shaped and blue-green foliage. They can be retained by annual hard pruning (height and spread given opposite are for pruned plants). Requires fertile soil that will not dry out.

2m / 1.2m

 leaf type   light preference   speed of growth   ease of growth

EUONYMUS FORTUNEI 'EMERALD 'N' GOLD'
SPINDLE TREE
CELASTRACEAE

A hardy shrub with glossy, bright green, gold-edged leaves. Leaves are particularly bright and colourful in spring; during cold spells in winter they become tinged with pink. Branches are spreading, but will climb if support is provided. Ideal for training through a tree or against a wall. Needs fertile, well-drained soil.

FATSIA JAPONICA
JAPANESE ARALIA
ARALIACEAE

A handsome, hardy or slightly tender shrub with a spreading nature. Has thick stems that bear large, bold, palmate, toothed leaves of deep, glossy green. In mid-autumn, round, drumstick heads of five-petalled tiny white flowers appear. A good specimen plant for a sheltered, shady position.

FREMONTODENDRON CALIFORNICUM
FLANNEL BUSH
STERCULIACEAE

A hardy shrub with a vigorous, upright nature which grows best in a sheltered position against a wall. Produces handsome dark leaves and shallow, saucer-shaped flowers which are bright golden yellow and large and showy. These are borne from late spring right through to autumn. Requires neutral to alkaline soil.

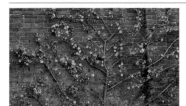

GARRYA ELLIPTICA 'JAMES ROOF'
SILK TASSEL BUSH
GARRYACEAE

Hardy shrub which grows best against a wall. It has leathery, green, oval leaves and in winter and early spring, the branches are beautifully decked with striking, silver-grey, trailing tassels — catkins which may reach up to 20cm (8in) long. Thrives in moderately fertile, well-drained soil.

GAULTHERIA MUCRONATA 'MULBERRY WINE' (SYN. PERNETTYA MUCRONATA)
PERNETTYA
ERICACEAE

A hardy shrub which produces bell-shaped white flowers in spring followed by deep purple-pink fruits. Only female varieties bear fruit, but a male variety grown close by is essential for pollination. Grow in acid, peaty, moist soil.

GENISTA LYDIA
BROOM
PAPILIONACEAE

A hardy dwarf shrub with spreading, arching, bright green branches and narrow leaves. In late spring and early summer, golden-yellow, pea-type flowers are carried in dense clusters. A lax habit makes this shrub particularly suitable for growing over rocks or retaining walls. Grow in light, fertile, well-drained soil.

↕ height and spread   ✱ feature of interest   � season of interest   *TREES AND SHRUBS* **D – G**

TREES AND SHRUBS

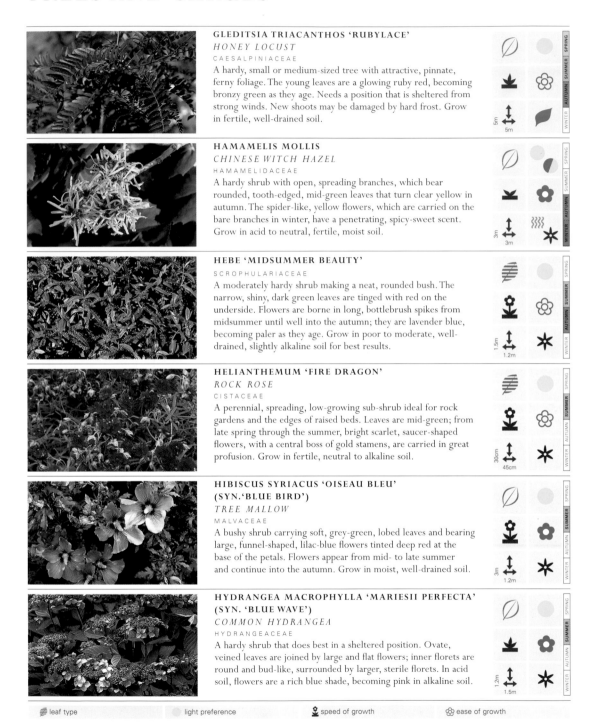

GLEDITSIA TRIACANTHOS 'RUBYLACE'
HONEY LOCUST
CAESALPINIACEAE

A hardy, small or medium-sized tree with attractive, pinnate, ferny foliage. The young leaves are a glowing ruby red, becoming bronzy green as they age. Needs a position that is sheltered from strong winds. New shoots may be damaged by hard frost. Grow in fertile, well-drained soil.

HAMAMELIS MOLLIS
CHINESE WITCH HAZEL
HAMAMELIDACEAE

A hardy shrub with open, spreading branches, which bear rounded, tooth-edged, mid-green leaves that turn clear yellow in autumn. The spider-like, yellow flowers, which are carried on the bare branches in winter, have a penetrating, spicy-sweet scent. Grow in acid to neutral, fertile, moist soil.

HEBE 'MIDSUMMER BEAUTY'
SCROPHULARIACEAE

A moderately hardy shrub making a neat, rounded bush. The narrow, shiny, dark green leaves are tinged with red on the underside. Flowers are borne in long, bottlebrush spikes from midsummer until well into the autumn; they are lavender blue, becoming paler as they age. Grow in poor to moderate, well-drained, slightly alkaline soil for best results.

HELIANTHEMUM 'FIRE DRAGON'
ROCK ROSE
CISTACEAE

A perennial, spreading, low-growing sub-shrub ideal for rock gardens and the edges of raised beds. Leaves are mid-green; from late spring through the summer, bright scarlet, saucer-shaped flowers, with a central boss of gold stamens, are carried in great profusion. Grow in fertile, neutral to alkaline soil.

HIBISCUS SYRIACUS 'OISEAU BLEU'
(SYN. 'BLUE BIRD')
TREE MALLOW
MALVACEAE

A bushy shrub carrying soft, grey-green, lobed leaves and bearing large, funnel-shaped, lilac-blue flowers tinted deep red at the base of the petals. Flowers appear from mid- to late summer and continue into the autumn. Grow in moist, well-drained soil.

HYDRANGEA MACROPHYLLA 'MARIESII PERFECTA'
(SYN. 'BLUE WAVE')
COMMON HYDRANGEA
HYDRANGEACEAE

A hardy shrub that does best in a sheltered position. Ovate, veined leaves are joined by large and flat flowers; inner florets are round and bud-like, surrounded by larger, sterile florets. In acid soil, flowers are a rich blue shade, becoming pink in alkaline soil.

leaf type   light preference   speed of growth   ease of growth

HYPERICUM X MOSERIANUM 'TRICOLOR'
ST. JOHN'S WORT
CLUSIACEAE

A spreading shrub with reddish shoots and ovate, green leaves, which can be variegated with three colours. Between summer and autumn, the plant produces cymes of yellow flowers. A good choice for a rock garden or a border. Needs moderately fertile, well-drained soil.

30cm / 60cm

ILEX AQUIFOLIUM 'J. C. VAN TOL'
HOLLY
AQUIFOLIACEAE

A hardy shrub or small tree, with very dark green, glossy leaves of a typical holly shape but with almost no spines. Clusters of small, starry, white flowers are followed by good crops of red berries. Unlike many hollies, it needs no pollinator in order to fruit well. Grow in moist but well-drained, humus-rich soil.

3m / 1.8m

LAURUS NOBILIS
SWEET BAY
LAURACEAE

Often grown as a standard or clipped topiary bush, the pointed, oval leaves are leathery and very dark green; they have a pungent aroma and are used as a culinary herb. Small, starry, cream flowers are carried in spring. Grow in moist, fertile and well-drained soil.

5m / 3m

LAVANDULA ANGUSTIFOLIA 'HIDCOTE'
LAVENDER
LAMIACEAE

A low shrub with narrow, grey leaves and spikes of tubular, purple-blue flowers in summer. All parts of the plant, especially the buds and flowers, are very fragrant, particularly when handled. Prune plants hard in spring to keep the growth shapely. Grow in moderately fertile, well-drained soil.

60cm / 60cm

MAGNOLIA STELLATA
STAR MAGNOLIA
MAGNOLIACEAE

A hardy, bushy shrub that bears many white, star-like, narrow-petalled flowers from early spring, when they spangle the bare branches. The form 'Rosea' has pink-tinged flowers. Leaves are lanceolate and mid-green. Grow in moist, well-drained soil.

2.5m / 3m

MAHONIA AQUIFOLIUM 'APOLLO'
OREGON GRAPE
BERBERIDACEAE

A hardy shrub with deep green, leathery, glossy leaves divided into prickly leaflets. In early spring, yellow flowers with an intense lily-of-the-valley fragrance are carried in dense, pyramidal clusters. They are followed by blue-black berries. Grow in fertile, moist but well-drained, humus-rich soil.

1m / 1.5m

⬍ height and spread   ✳ feature of interest   ▮▮▮ season of interest   *TREES AND SHRUBS* **G – M**

TREES AND SHRUBS

MALUS 'JOHN DOWNIE'
CRAB APPLE
ROSACEAE

A small, hardy tree providing excellent value. It bears a profusion of white apple blossom in spring, and attractive, plum-sized, elongated crab apples in summer and autumn. These are yellow, flushed with orange and red, and make an excellent crab apple jelly. Grow in moderately fertile, moist, well-drained soil.

MYRTUS COMMUNIS
MYRTLE
MYRTACEAE

A rather tender shrub with small, deep green, glossy leaves, which are aromatic when crushed. In summer, fragrant, saucer-shaped white flowers are produced. A sprig of myrtle is a traditional addition to a bride's bouquet. Grow in fertile, moist but well-drained soil.

NANDINA DOMESTICA 'FIREPOWER'
HEAVENLY BAMBOO
BERBERIDACEAE

A dwarf shrub with colourful foliage, particularly through winter when it takes on burnished shades of red and orange. The leaves are divided into leaflets, which are tinged red when young and open to a pale green in summer. A sheltered site helps stop the loss of winter foliage. Grow in moist, well-drained soil.

OSMANTHUS DELAVAYI
OLEACEAE

A hardy, bushy shrub with glossy, dark green, ovate, toothed leaves. In mid-spring it carries large numbers of tubular white flowers, which have a strong, sweet fragrance. A position sheltered from cold winds will give the best results. Grow in fertile, well-drained soil.

PACHYSANDRA TERMINALIS
BUXACEAE

A hardy, spreading perennial with dark green, diamond-shaped, toothed leaves carried in whorls towards the ends of the stems. In late spring, small spikes of white flowers with prominent stamens appear at the tips of the shoots. A good choice for ground cover. Needs acid soil, moist but well drained.

PHILADELPHUS 'BELLE ETOILE'
MOCK ORANGE
HYDRANGEACEAE

A hardy shrub making strong, upright growth with light green, veined leaves and white, cup-shaped, four-petalled flowers in early summer. These have a purple stain at the base of the petals and prominent, golden stamens; they are noted for their strong, sweet, orange-blossom scent. Grow in any soil.

≣ leaf type   ● light preference   ♣ speed of growth   ✿ ease of growth

PHLOX SUBULATA 'TEMISKAMING'
MOSS PHLOX
POLEMONIACEAE

A hardy, low-growing sub-shrub particularly suitable for rockeries and walls. Linear, light green leaves are joined by a mass of flat-faced, open flowers on short stems in summer. 'Temiskaming' is bright magenta; there are also pink- and lilac-flowered varieties. Grow in fertile, well-drained soil.

PHORMIUM 'DAZZLER'
NEW ZEALAND FLAX
AGAVACEAE

A moderately hardy perennial plant producing a clump of upright, sword-like leaves striped in shades of purple, pink and yellow – a very striking, architectural specimen. Panicles of red flowers may be produced on tall stems in summer. Needs some winter protection in cold areas. Likes fertile, well-drained soil.

PHOTINIA X FRASERI 'RED ROBIN'
ROSACEAE

An upright shrub or small tree grown for its foliage and flowers. Leaves begin life bright red and age to dark green. In mid- and late spring, the plant produces small white flowers. This is a good plant to grow as a specimen in a shrub border or against a wall. Choose soil that is moist but well drained and fertile.

PHYGELIUS X RECTUS 'AFRICAN QUEEN'
SCROPHULARIACEAE

A moderately hardy sub-shrub, which is usually grown as an herbaceous perennial. A bushy plant with lanceolate, deep green leaves. Tall stems carry open spires of tubular, slightly downward-curving, pale red flowers with yellow throats. Best in a sheltered position. Grow in a soil that is fertile, moist and well drained.

PIERIS JAPONICA 'GRAYSWOOD'
ERICACEAE

A hardy shrub of very compact growth, with small, narrow, dark green, pointed leaves. In spring, spreading, branching panicles of small, white, urn-shaped, pendent flowers are freely carried. 'Grayswood' is tolerant of shady conditions. Good for a border or as a specimen plant. Grow in acid soil that is humus-rich, moderately fertile and well drained.

PIPTANTHUS NEPALENSIS
EVERGREEN LABURNUM
PAPILIONACEAE

From a genus of shrubs indigenous to China and the Himalayas, an upright plant with palmate, dark green leaves. In late spring and early summer, it produces small yellow flowers. A good plant for training against a wall. Likes fertile, well-drained soil.

| height and spread | feature of interest | season of interest | *TREES AND SHRUBS* **M – P** |

TREES AND SHRUBS

PITTOSPORUM TENUIFOLIUM 'TOM THUMB'

PITTOSPORACEAE

A moderately hardy or slightly tender shrub, this compact variety makes a neat, rounded outline. The ovate leaves, with lightly waved margins, are pale green, becoming a deep purple-red as they age. In summer, purple, cup-shaped flowers are carried, but they are not particularly showy. Grow in fertile soil that is moist but well drained.

PRUNUS INCISA 'KOJO-NO-MAI'

FUJI CHERRY

ROSACEAE

An ideal specimen tree. In spring, the branches are loaded with small, pinkish-white, fluttering blossoms; its common name translates as 'dance of the butterflies'. Blooms are followed by fresh green, toothed leaves that turn bright orange and scarlet in autumn. Likes moist, well-drained fertile soil.

PRUNUS LUSITANICA 'VARIEGATA'

PORTUGUESE LAUREL

ROSACEAE

A bushy shrub or tree with red stalks and ovate, glossy, dark green leaves. In early summer, the plant will produce cup-shaped white flowers, which are fragrant. These are superseded by cherry-like, red fruit. Grow in moist, well-drained, fertile soil.

PYRACANTHA 'WATERERI'

FIRETHORN

ROSACEAE

The spiny, strong-growing, woody stems bear small, ovate, bright green leaves, and in early summer, a froth of creamy-white blossoms in domed heads. These are followed by bunches of long-lasting, bright scarlet berries. Grows well when trained as a wall shrub. Grow in fertile, well-drained soil.

RHODODENDRON 'KIRIN'

AZALEA

ERICACEAE

A hardy shrub with deep green, ovate or rounded leaves on spreading, compact stems. The striking, silver-rose flowers appear in spring, their 'hose-in-hose' form consisting of one flower within another. One of many dozens of hybrid azalea varieties in a wide range of colours. Grow in rich, moist soil.

ROBINIA HISPIDA

ROSE ACACIA

PAPILIONACEAE

A hardy, suckering shrub of arching habit, with bristly stems and ferny, deep green, graceful leaves. In late spring, drooping racemes of deep, rosy-pink flowers are produced. Can be grown as a small tree when grafted on to a single stem; otherwise best as a wall shrub. Will tolerate most soils.

≋ leaf type   ● light preference   ♁ speed of growth   ⚙ ease of growth

ROSA 'SWEET DREAM'
ROSE

ROSACEAE

A hardy, compact-growing shrub that has been bred as a 'patio rose', ideal for growing in containers. The small leaves are bright, glossy green, and the small, peach-coloured double flowers are carried in clusters in summer and autumn. Grow in fertile, humus-rich, moist but well-drained soil.

37cm
37cm

ROSMARINUS OFFICINALIS 'SEVERN SEA'
ROSEMARY

LAMIACEAE

A moderately hardy shrub with aromatic, needle-like, silver-green leaves on arching stems and very bright blue, hooded flowers in summer. This variety is most reliable in a warm, sheltered position. Rosemary is widely used as a culinary herb. Grow in well-drained, poor to moderate soil.

60cm
1m

RUTA GRAVEOLENS 'JACKMAN'S BLUE'
RUE

RUTACEAE

Has very finely cut, steely blue foliage with a pungent, bitter, coconut aroma. Rue should not be used in cooking. Pale yellow flowers are produced in summer, but are often removed to prevent them detracting from the foliage. Grow in very well-drained soil.

60cm
60cm

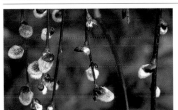

SALIX CAPREA 'KILMARNOCK'
KILMARNOCK WILLOW

SALICACEAE

A hardy shrub, the Kilmarnock willow has strongly weeping branches and forms an attractive small tree, especially when the soft, silver 'pussy-willow' catkins are present in late winter and early spring. Later in the spring the catkins become golden as the anthers become evident. Grow in any moist, well-drained soil.

1.3m
1.5m

SALVIA OFFICINALIS 'TRICOLOR'
TRICOLOUR SAGE

LAMIACEAE

Striking oblong, wrinkled, aromatic leaves, which are grey-green flushed with irregular purple, pink and cream markings. Prune plants hard in spring to keep them compact. Take cuttings and overwinter them under cover to provide replacements in case of winter losses. Grow in light, fertile soil.

45cm
60cm

SAMBUCUS RACEMOSA 'PLUMOSA AUREA'
CUT-LEAVED ELDER

CAPRIFOLICEAE

A hardy shrub with leaves divided into slender leaflets with finely cut, fringed margins. The leaves are a beautiful, rich, soft gold shade. Panicles of creamy flowers are followed by red berries but this shrub is grown mainly for its foliage effects. Grow in moist, but well-drained, fertile, humus-rich soil.

1.8m
1.8m

---

 height and spread   ✳ feature of interest   season of interest   *TREES AND SHRUBS* **P – S**

TREES AND SHRUBS

SARCOCOCCA CONFUSA
SWEET BOX
BUXACEAE

Branches bear small, glossy, dark green, pointed leaves, and, in late winter, small, white, very fragrant flowers, followed by round, black berries. *Sarcococca* is a useful, shade-tolerant shrub, and the flowering branches are good for cutting for the house. Grow in fertile, humus-rich, moist but well-drained soil.

SKIMMIA JAPONICA 'RUBELLA'
RUTACEAE

A shrub with leathery, deep green, lance-shaped leaves that have a fine red rim and are aromatic when crushed. Flower buds form in autumn in dense, domed panicles: they are bright, rosy red and persist through the winter months. In spring, they open to starry white flowers. This is a male form which does not produce berries. Likes moist, well-drained fertile soil.

SPIRAEA JAPONICA 'GOLDFLAME'
ROSACEAE

A clump-forming shrub with sharply toothed, bronze leaves when young, which turn green with age. In summer, it produces corymbs of dark pink flowers. A good plant for a rock garden or for producing informal hedging. This is a plant that will appreciate soil that is moist but well drained and fertile.

SYRINGA MEYERI 'PALIBIN'
LILAC
OLEACEAE

A hardy shrub with oval, mid-green leaves on bushy stems. Panicles of flowers are produced in late spring and early summer, made up of tubular, lilac-pink blooms with a distinctive, sweet fragrance. 'Palibin' makes a much more compact shrub than most common lilac varieties. Grow in fertile, humus-rich soil.

THYMUS X CITRIODORUS 'SILVER QUEEN'
LEMON-SCENTED THYME
LAMIACEAE

A low-growing, spreading sub-shrub with very small, oval, aromatic leaves. The foliage is pale grey-green strongly marked with silvery white; clusters of small, pale lilac flowers open in midsummer. A popular culinary herb, with a warm, citrus scent. Grow in well-drained, neutral to alkaline soil.

TRACHYCARPUS FORTUNEI
CHUSAN PALM
ARECACEAE

A moderately hardy tree with large, fan-shaped, deeply divided, mid-green palm leaves on long, toothed stalks. It grows slowly, eventually producing a stout, fibrous trunk. Makes an excellent, exotic-looking specimen plant for a sheltered spot, though usually expensive to buy. Grow in well-drained, fertile soil.

≣ leaf type   ● light preference   ⚵ speed of growth   ⊛ ease of growth

VIBURNUM X BODNANTENSE 'DAWN'
CAPRIFOLIACEAE

A hardy, upright-growing shrub that carries clusters of tubular, pink-flushed, white flowers on bare branches throughout the winter. They are especially numerous in mild spells, and have a very strong, pleasant fragrance. The oval, toothed leaves which follow are bronze tinted, opening to mid-green. Grow in almost any moist but well-drained soil.

VIBURNUM TINUS 'EVE PRICE'
LAURUSTINUS
CAPRIFOLIACEAE

A hardy shrub, compact and bushy. It has oval, glossy, dark green leaves and bears numerous flattened heads of pink-tinted, white, star-shaped flowers throughout the winter. These are followed by clusters of blue berries. Easy going and adaptable. Grow in moist but well-drained soil.

VINCA MAJOR
GREATER PERIWINKLE
APOCYNACEAE

A hardy sub-shrub of creeping, arching growth. It has pointed, glossy, deep green leaves on wiry, vigorous stems, and from mid-spring to autumn bears numerous bright blue, tubular, flat-faced flowers. Makes good ground cover, though it is invasive. Likes almost any soil, apart from very dry.

VINCA MINOR
LESSER PERIWINKLE
APOCYNACEAE

A low-growing, prostrate shrub, good for growing over structures like a pergola or arch. It has lance-shaped, dark green leaves, and from mid-spring to autumn, blue, purple or white flowers are produced. Likes almost any soil, in full sunlight for best flowering.

WEIGELA 'VICTORIA'
CAPRIFOLIACEAE

A hardy shrub with deep green, oval leaves flushed dark purple. The tubular flowers are rosy red, carried in dense clusters in early summer, and sometimes again later in the season. 'Victoria' makes a compact bush, ideal for smaller gardens. Grow in fertile, well-drained soil.

YUCCA FLACCIDA 'IVORY'
AGAVACEAE

A hardy shrub producing a large rosette of narrow, sword-shaped, blue-green leaves, which have thread-like, curling filaments at their margins. From midsummer, tall spikes bearing showy panicles of bell-shaped, creamy-white, green-flushed flowers are produced. An impressive, exotic-looking specimen plant. Grow in any well-drained soil.

↕ height and spread ✱ feature of interest ▭▭▭ season of interest *TREES AND SHRUBS S – Y*

GLOSSARY

ACCLIMATIZATION: Process of preparing a plant for moving outside after it has been growing indoors, usually by taking it outside for increasingly extended periods.

ALPINE: A plant that in its natural mountain habitat grows above the uppermost limit of trees. More colloquially, plants that are suitable for rock gardens are called alpines.

ANNUAL: A plant that grows from seed, flowers and dies within the same year. Some half-hardy perennial plants are used as annuals, that is, they die off in the winter.

ANTHER: Pollen-bearing part of the stamen of a flower.

AQUATIC PLANT: A plant that lives totally or partly submerged in water.

BEDDING PLANTS: Plants that are set out for a temporary spring or summer display and discarded at the end of the season.

BIENNIAL: A plant raised from seed that makes its initial growth in one year and flowers during the following one, then dies.

BULB: An underground food storage organ formed of fleshy, modified leaves that enclose a dormant shoot.

CALYX: The outer and protective part of a flower. It is usually green and is very apparent in roses.

COMPOST: Vegetable waste from kitchens, as well as soft parts of garden plants, which is encouraged to decompose and to form a material that can be dug into soil or used to create a mulch around plants.

CORM: An underground storage organ formed of a swollen stem base, for example, a gladiolus.

CULTIVAR: A shortened term for 'cultivated variety' that indicates a variety raised in cultivation. Strictly speaking, most modern varieties are cultivars, but the term variety is still widely used because it is familiar to most gardeners.

CUTTING: A section of plant which is detached and encouraged to form roots and stems to provide a new independent plant. Cuttings may be taken from roots, stems or leaves.

DEAD-HEADING: The removal of a faded flower head to prevent the formation of seeds and to encourage the development of further flowers.

DECIDUOUS: Plants that lose their leaves during the winter are referred to as deciduous.

DORMANT: When a plant is alive but is making no growth, it is called dormant. The dormant period is usually the winter.

EVERGREEN: Plants that appear to be green throughout the year and not to lose their leaves are called ever-green. In reality, however, they shed some of their leaves throughout the year, while producing others.

FRIABLE: Soil that is crumbly and light and easily worked. It especially applies to soil being prepared as a seedbed in spring.

HALF-HARDY: A plant that can withstand fairly low temperatures, but needs protection from frost.

HALF-HARDY ANNUAL: An annual that is sown in gentle warmth in a greenhouse in spring, the seedlings being transferred to wider spacings in pots or boxes. The plants are placed in a garden or container only when all risk of frost has passed.

HARDEN OFF: To gradually accustom plants raised under cover to cooler conditions so that they can be planted outside.

HARDY: A plant that is able to survive outdoors in winter. In the case of some rock-garden plants, good drainage is essential to ensure their survival.

HERB: A plant that is grown for its aromatic qualities and can often be used in cooking or medicinally.

HERBACEOUS PERENNIAL: A plant with no woody tissue that lives for several years. It may be deciduous or evergreen.

HYBRID: A cross between two different species, varieties or genera of plants.

LOAM: Friable topsoil.

MULCHING: Covering the soil around plants with well-decayed organic material such as garden compost, peat or, in the case of rock garden plants, stone chippings or 6mm (¼in) shingle.

NEUTRAL: Soil that is neither acid nor alkaline, with a pH of 7.0, is said to be neutral. Most plants grow in a pH of about 6.5.

PEAT: A naturally occurring substance formed from partly rotted organic material in water-logged soils, used as a growing medium and soil additive.

PERENNIAL: Any plant that lives for three or more years is called a perennial.

PERGOLA: An open timber structure made up of linked arches.

POTTING COMPOST: Traditionally, a compost formed of loam, sharp sand and peat, fertilizers and chalk. The ratio of the ingredients is altered according to whether the compost is used for sowing seeds, potting-up or repotting plants into larger containers. Recognition of the environmental importance of conserving peat beds has led to many modern composts being formed of other organic materials, such as coir or shredded bark.

PRICKING OFF: Transplanting seedlings from the container in which they were sown to one where they are more widely spaced.

RAISED BED: A raised area, usually encircled by a dry-stone wall. Rock garden plants can be grown both in the raised bed and the wall.

RHIZOME: An underground or partly buried horizontal stem. They can be slender or fleshy. They act as storage organs and perpetuate plants from one season to another.

SCREE BED: An area formed of small stones, together with a few large rocks, often positioned at the base of a rock garden.

SEED LEAVES: The first leaves that develop on a seedling, which are coarser and more robust than the true leaves.

SEMI-EVERGREEN: A plant that may keep some of its leaves in a reasonably mild winter.

SINK GARDENS: Old stone sinks partly filled with drainage material and then with freely draining compost. They are planted with miniature conifers and bulbs, as well as small rock garden plants, and are usually displayed on patios.

SPECIES ROSE: A term for a wild rose or one of its near relatives.

SPECIMEN PLANT: A plant that is attractive enough to be grown on its own rather than in a bed or border with other plants.

STAMEN: The male part of a flower.

STANDARD: A tree or shrub trained to form a rounded head of branches at the top of a clear stem.

SUB-SHRUB: Small and spreading shrub with a woody base. It differs from normal shrubs in that when grown in temperate regions its upper stems and shoots die back during winter.

TENDER: A plant which will not tolerate cold conditions is referred to as tender.

TILTH: Friable topsoil in which seeds are sown. It also acts as a mulch on the surface of soil, helping to reduce the loss of moisture from the soil's surface.

TOPSOIL: The uppermost fertile layer of soil that is suitable for plant growth.

TUBER: A swollen, thickened and fleshy stem or root. Some tubers are swollen roots (dahlia), while others are swollen stems (potato). They serve as storage organs and help to perpetuate plants from one season to another.

VARIEGATED: Usually applied to leaves and used to describe a state of having two or more colours.

VARIETY: A naturally occurring variation of a species that retains its characteristics when propagated. The term is often used for cultivars.

INDEX

ACKNOWLEDGEMENTS

t *top* **b** *below* **l** *left* **r** *right* **Directory a–f**, *starting from top*

Liz Eddison 4,16t, 18t, 21, 22, 26 32r, 34r, 36l, 64–65/Chelsea Physic Garden 38r
Designer: Ruth Chivers, Hampton Court 99–7/Natural & Oriental Water Garden 41r
Designer David Platt, Chelsea 96 34l/Designer: Georgina Steeds 28, 36r
Designer Geoffrey Whitten, Chelsea 99 12t;
The Garden Picture Library/David Askham 68d/Mark Bolton 39r/Eric Crichton 33l/Ron
Evans 60/Sunnvia Harte 37r/Neil Holmes 40r, 104b/Lamontage 39l
JS Sira 17/Jerry Pavia 88f/David Russell 42/Ron Sutherland 13, 14b, 18b, 19, 20b, 23
Brigitte Thomas 54/Designer Geoffrey Whitten 32l/Steven Wooster 40l & 62, 56;
John Glover 1, 2, 5, 6, 10–11, 14t, 15, 16b, 20t, 30–31, 33r, 35l,r, 37l, 40l, 52, 58, 62
Designer: Karen Maskell, Hampton Court 99 38l
Designer: Mark Walker, Chelsea 96 12bl;
Lucy Huntington 24;
Peter McHoy 68a,b, 69a,b,d, 70a,b,e,f, 71b,c,d, 72a,b,d, 73b,c,d,e,f, 74a,b,d,
75c,d, 76a,b,c,de,f, 77a,b,c,d,e, 78b,e,f, 79b,c,d,ef, 80a,b,c,d,e,f, 81a,b,c,d,e,f, 82a,c,
83a,b,d,e, 84a,b,c,d,e,f, 85b,c,e, 86a,b,c,e, 87a,c,d,e, 88b,c,d,e, 89b,c,d,e,f, 90b,d,e,
91b,f, 92c,d, 93b,d, 94b,d, f, 95b,c,e, 96a,f, 97a,c,d,e,f, 98a,c,d,f, 99a,c,e,f, 100b,c,d,e,
101c,d,e, 102a,c,d,e,f, 103a,b,d,f, 104a,f, 105a,c,d,e,f, 106b,d,f, 107a,b,c,f;
The Harry Smith Collection 68c,e, 69c,e,f, 70c,d, 71a,e,f, 72c,e,f, 73a, 74c,e,f,
75b,e,f, 77f, 78a,d,c, 79a, 82b,d,e,f, 83c,f, 85a,d,f, 86d,f, 87b, f, 88a, 89a, 90a,f,
91a,c,d,e, 92a,b,e,f, 93a,c,e,f, 94a,c,d,e, 95a,d,f, 96b,d,e, 97b, 98b,e, 99d, 100a,f,
101a,b,f, 102b, 103c,e, 104c,d,e, 105b, 106a,e, 107d,e;
David Squire 90c, 96c, 99b, 106c.